THE MANSIONS

ALSO BY DANIEL TOBIN

THE MANSIONS

DANIEL TOBIN

FOUR WAY BOOKS
TRIBECA

LIBRARY OF CONGRESS CATALOGING-IN-PUBLICATION DATA

Names: Tobin, Daniel, author.

Title: The mansions / by Daniel Tobin.

Description: New York : Four Way Books, [2023]

Identifiers: LCCN 2023004474 (print) | LCCN 2023004475 (ebook) | ISBN
  9781954245600 (trade paperback) | ISBN 9781954245617 (ebook)

Subjects: LCGFT: Poetry.

Classification: LCC PS3570.O289 M36 2023 (print) | LCC PS3570.O289
  (ebook) | DDC 811/.54--dc23/eng/20230210

LC record available at https://lccn.loc.gov/2023004474

LC ebook record available at https://lccn.loc.gov/2023004475

This book is manufactured in the United States of America and printed on acid-free paper.

Four Way Books is a not-for-profit literary press. We are grateful for the assistance
we receive from individual donors, public arts agencies, and private foundations
including the NEA, NEA Cares, Literary Arts Emergency Fund, and the
New York State Council on the Arts, a state agency.

We are a proud member of the Community of Literary Magazines and Presses.

CONTENTS

PREFACE

In his 1836 essay, "Nature," Ralph Waldo Emerson wrote, "To speak truly, few adult persons can see nature. Most persons do not see the sun. At least they have a very superficial seeing. The sun illuminates only the eye of the man, but shines into the eye and heart of the child." What Emerson means, or part of what he means, is that familiarity and long habit make it difficult for us to see things as they are. Were a single blade of grass found on Mars, the world would shake, yet we look on millions of blades of grass without a thought. Were a single flower found on the moon, it would change our lives forever, yet we see untold numbers of flowers and feel nothing.

Earth is, so far as we know, the only place in the universe where there is life. How is it, then, that we hold life so lightly? If you are reading this, you are a miracle. For it is nothing short of a miracle—whether one believes in the divine or not—that on this lone rock, whirling around a fiery ball of gas, so much of life should flourish, while existing nowhere else. The odds against any life ever forming are, literally, astronomical, and yet there is life, here and now, and you are alive. Better still, there is life all around you, more life than anyone could ever see or know, more than anyone has ever seen or known: hence, we continue to discover new species, new lifeforms.

To read Daniel Tobin's tripartite poem, *The Mansions*, is to feel a frisson of life's grandeur, of its majesty and mystery. Emerson writes that looking at the stars awakens "a certain reverence" in us, and reading *The Mansions* may do the same, may awaken in us a heightened awareness of how unlikely, how rare and precious, how sacred all life is, and how unthinkably superabundant. As John 14:2 has it, "There are many mansions in my father's house."

Among the many mansions in the magnificent house of Tobin's poem, we find aesthetics merge with biography and biology, cosmology and genetics, ethics and geology, history and geography, ontogeny, phylogeny, quantum physics, and topography. We find English alongside Aramaic, French, German, Italian, Latin, Portuguese, and Spanish. We find Buddhism, Judaism, Hinduism, Gnosticism, Positivism, Marxism, Manicheism, and Catholicism, as well as Greco-Roman mythology. In this commodious house there is room for historical figures—Charlie Chaplin, Pope Pius XII, and Leon Trotsky—to rub shoulders with philosophers such as Simone de Beauvoir, Gabriel Marcel, Nietzsche, Pascal, Plato, Rousseau, and Gustave Thibon. Here the great minds of science—Niels Bohr, Einstein, Kurt Gödel, Hubble, Mendel, Newton, Poincaré, and Schrödinger—mingle with divines and mystics such as St. Augustine, St. Thomas Aquinas, St. Francis of Assisi, Nicholas of Cusa, and Jan van Ruysbroeck. Here artists—Praxiteles, Bosh, Botticelli, da Vinci, de Hooch, Giorgione, Goya, Magritte, Picasso, Lucile Swan, and Watteau—gather with poets: Donne, Goethe, Heaney, Herbert, Li Po, Molière, Rilke, Stein, Paul Valéry, and Yeats. Tobin's book teems with life.

And yet, *The Mansions* is no formless chaos: far from it. The poem consists of three canticles: "From Nothing," "This Broken Symmetry," and "At the Grave of Teilhard de Chardin." Each canticle, or section, consists of thirty-three cantos, or subsections. Each canto consists of twenty-four lines, divided into eight tercets. Another canto of twenty-four lines, the 100th canto of the book, is broken into four sections that appear before and after each canticle in fragments of six lines divided into couplets.

In its arrangement, then, *The Mansions* intentionally recalls the *Divina Commedia* of Dante Alighieri, itself broken into three canticles—*Inferno, Purgatorio*, and *Paradiso*—and containing 100 cantos, also divided into tercets. Dante's *Commedia* synthesized all of the most up-to-date science and theology of its time, harmonizing the two into a single vision that informs his masterpiece; staggeringly, Tobin's poem attempts a similar feat in our own time, a time in which science and theology often seem impossible to reconcile.

The first canticle, "From Nothing," centers on the life of Georges Lemaître, a Jesuit priest from Belgium, who was also a groundbreaking mathematician and theoretical physicist. It was Lemaître who first theorized the "Big Bang," and his work also anticipated the discovery of black holes and the cosmic microwave. Devoted both to science and to Christian mysticism, "physics and faith," Lemaître's life seemed to move in two divergent directions; however, each devotion informed the other. To render such complication artistically, Tobin brilliantly configures this canticle around what Einstein called *spukhafte Fernwirkung*, or "spooky action at a distance," and through this figuration harmonizes the interplay between physics and faith in Lemaître's life.

The second canticle, "This Broken Symmetry," focuses on the revolutionary Albigensian mystic, Simone Weil. Beginning at Weil's grave in Bybrook Cemetery, Kent, and concluding with her yet unborn at her grandmother's house on the Rue de Paradis in Paris, this canticle takes its formal principle from Weil's concept of decreation. The third canticle, "At the Grave of Teilhard de Chardin," concerns the titular priest-cum-scientist-and-theologian. Beginning with a monologue spoken by de Chardin's gravestone, this canticle moves from cantos spoken by inanimate objects, through monologues spoken by those who knew de Chardin, to the concluding eleven cantos, which are in the voice of the contemporary poet speaking in propria persona. In this movement, the canticle embodies de Chardin's notion of life's spiritualizing evolution from inanimate matter toward the "Omega Point." However, as in de Chardin's thought the Omega Point is synonymous with the Christian Logos—both Alpha and Omega, beginning and end—so the fragment of the 100th canto, appearing after this final canticle, points back toward the fragment preceding the first canticle. The end is the beginning.

To behold such towering formal structure is dizzying, akin to looking on the flying buttress of a great cathedral. And there is not room enough in this preface even to mention the painstaking detail of each canto. For instance, in the penultimate canto of the final canticle, Tobin presents a poem that works like a double-helix: one can read the left column as a poem, the right column as a poem, and the two together as a third poem. Oh, and the final eleven cantos of *The Mansions* also happen to take on the form of *terza rima*—that form invented by Dante for his *Commedia*—for good measure.

In short, Daniel Tobin's *The Mansions* is nothing less than a wonder. In its compendious learning, its consummate artistry, and its spiritual wisdom, this poem inspires genuine awe, and it challenges the reader to think more broadly and more acutely, to feel more profoundly, and to live life more attentively. In these days, as so many of us feel darkness growing all around us, Tobin's poem may serve us as a guide and lead us to a place where we're able *riveder le stelle*, "to see again the stars," as Dante does upon emerging from the Inferno, where we may see again deep in our hearts, as children do, the dazzle of the sun.

RYAN WILSON
WASHINGTON, D.C.
FEBRUARY 1ST, 2022

THE MANSIONS

Now, when each of the stars, which were necessary to the creation of time, had come to its proper orbit, and they had become living creatures having bodies fastened by vital chains, and learned their appointed task... they revolved, some in larger and some in lesser orbit...

PLATO, Timaeus

MANSION (n.) from the Latin *mansionem* (nominative *mansion*) "a staying, a remaining, night quarters, station," noun of action from past participle stem of *manere* "to stay, abide" (from PIE root *men*, "to remain"). The word was also used in Middle English as "a stop or stage on a journey," hence probably the astrological sense "temporary home."

...this sudden stirring, like birds before
an earthquake, then the explosion—

a fluency of wine in water, white streak
across a white vault of sky where the tunnel

opens to Bright Abounding, its utter light,
fleet release, ecstatic, unutterable, before...

ONE

From Nothing

*And to one God says: Come
to me by numbers and
figures: see my beauty
in the angles between
stars, in the equations
of my kingdom...*

*And to another:
I am the bush burning
at the center of
your existence...*

R.S. THOMAS, "MEDITATIONS"

Georges Lemaître was a Belgian mathematician, theoretical physicist, and Jesuit priest whose insights during the 1930s and 1940s provided solutions to physical problems stemming from Einstein's general theory of relativity and quantum mechanics that Einstein himself did not foresee. Though a lesser-known figure in cosmology, he was the first to develop a theory of an expanding universe through the explosion of a "primeval atom," what has become known popularly as "the big bang." He was the first to recognize the validity of the cosmological constant (lambda) as a gravitationally repulsive force that explains the current acceleration of cosmic expansion, and the first to offer mathematical solutions that anticipated the discovery of black holes. He envisioned, in short, the most scientifically robust theory of the universe before the discovery of cosmic microwave background radiation, the CMB, which he predicted, as well as the theory of inflation that has emerged from "big bang" theory. While there is sublimity in Lemaître's scientific and mathematical genius, his life also intersects intimately and crucially with the twentieth century's most profound historical and human catastrophes. A devotee of the fourteenth century Flemish mystic, Jan van Ruysbroeck, Lemaître was likewise pioneer of computer programming and modeling. Georges Lemaître died on the cusp of the summer solstice, a week after being told of Penzias and Wilson's discovery of the CMB, the fossil light that is quietly and indelibly present in all quarters of the sky.

The Most Ancient Light in the Most Ancient Sky

We may speak of this event as a beginning; I do not say a creation...
Any preexistence of the universe has a metaphysical character.
Physically, everything happens as if the theoretical zero was really
a beginning. The question if it was really a beginning or rather a
creation, something started from nothing, is a philosophical question
which cannot be settled by physical or astronomical considerations.

GEORGES LEMAÎTRE

(Fountain)

To figure from nothing, holiness in perihelion:
though one must not proclaim it, but let the matter
spin along its poles into the bright entanglements,

like two particles of light flung to opposite zones,
and still the one moves with and how the other moves—
love's choreography in the elegance of the dance.

Though maybe it's more like matter and antimatter,
the one canceling the other in a blinding negation,
number and *noumen* locked in their separate estates.

You would not collapse them to a point's white heat,
but kept them before you, your physics and your faith,
the divergent roads with their singular horizon

where the radius of space converges into zero,
where what was, is, will be waxes without boundary
into seed and sand grain, a Cepheid luster of eyes—

news of the minor signature keyed from everywhere,
the primal radiation, omnipresent, the prodigal
wave arriving from its Now that has no yesterday,

the proof of your calculus, the tour of the expanse:
"The evolution of the universe might be compared
to a display of fireworks that has just ended,

some few red wisps, ashes and smoke. So, we stand
on a well-cooled cinder to see the fading of suns,
to glimpse a vanished brilliance, the origin of worlds."

(Origin)

A little sand, a little soda, a little lime once used
to embalm the dead, and out of black hole and kiln
the molten bubble gathers like honey on a dipper

for the blower to stretch breath into glass, the pipe
a silent horn shaping the form with its emptiness
to be marvered and mandrelled, jacked and lathed.

In your father's factory the vessels anneal, neat rows
of flagons, jars, mould blown, ribbed and decorated,
every glinted edge and pattern the fire will destroy

so the life foreseen becomes a retrospect foreknown:
the char-black rolling country of the Pays Noir
from which your people came—the smelting works

and coal pits, gas, slag-heap, pickaxe and sump.
He rose from all that, and rose again to make good
for the losses, for his laborers, as though justice

were the standard candle he followed in the dark,
or the hidden vein in a seam of earth that opens
on a vault where monstrance lifts from the monstrous.

In the photographer's studio your mother nestles you
on folded cloth, an heir of miners and weavers,
the scene a tapestry of hills and fields and settling sky.

You could be a girl in your frilled gown, or Rilke,
your eyes as bright and lenient, your right hand
gesturing outward, the left already figuring sums.

(Fiat)

In the Cathedral Saint-Michel, the chancel window
pours down its lucid spectrum across the altar.
The priest in green chasuble for Ordinary Time

bows before the tabernacle, paten, chalice, *Agnus Dei*.
Uniformly you sit among the pews and schoolboys.
Latin and incense commingle beneath the nave.

The altar servers in their chiaroscuro—white surplice,
black soutane—move in consort to cross and ciborium.
Is it now that you sense the certainty of your calling?

Or had it haunted you nights with your schoolbooks
even back in Charleroi, in the halls of Sacré-Cœur:
calculation and consecration, geometry and God?

"There is nothing I think in all of physical reality
more abstruse than the doctrine of the Trinity,"
you would write years later, your primeval quantum

inflating to millennia, into weeks and days:
if only every life, like quires in a Book of Hours,
could unfold from vellum, unique and indelible.

In the glittering fan the priest lifts host and chalice,
bread and wine to body and blood, as though a switch
flickered at the bottom of things, its sizzling foam,

with a word accidence into essence alchemized.
While outside immaculate gardens begin to bloom
in riots of light, pallets of flesh, stained glass blazoning.

(De Rerum)
Georges Lemaître

"A red flare broadcasts its annunciation over the Salient,
Ypres in the half-light of morning, an unnatural silence
broken by the screech of shrapnel shell and howitzer,

machine guns spattering the parapets of No Man's Land.
Horrible enough the slaughter, hand to hand, house to house,
in Lombartzyde—bayonet, rifle shot, the blood in my nails.

We've opened the sea sluices to hold back their onslaught,
Louvain burned, this one strip left of free Belgium.
Now these crater fields, the men mown down in swathes.

Why is it, O my Precious Christ, we do this to each other,
crouching in transverse, trench, the barbed, deadlocked lines,
who might have joined like harvesters among hedge and fold?

A hiss, and from enemy dugouts the strange cloud curls
in waves, grayish, yellow to green, darkest at the bottom.
And I know we are in a biblical plague, the men fumbling

for bits of flannel, cotton pads, the gassed in spasm, clawing
at their throats, their eyes, vomiting, crawling off to die—
the way the forsaken do in Bruegel's *The Triumph of Death,*

its black plumes of smoke and burning cities, its scythes
and armies, skeletal, their coffin lid shields, the slit throats,
wagonloads of skulls, that dog nibbling a dead child's face.

On the ravaged plain, a cauldron of torture and carnage
like ours with its mangles, stumps, stench, and splintered trees,
the Cross still rises skyward, Death hammering the plinth."

(Parallax)

To have lived inside wrath: *Croix de Guerre:* the continent
a slaughterhouse. To have borne it, strafes, gas, liquid fire,
to have come through—by what turn of Catherine wheel,

by what hand? While other minds were ground to chaff.
You calculating the cosines of targets, trajectories,
in the rare calm reading Poincaré in trench and redoubt,

time synchronized with space in telegraph and meridian,
cables under crisscrossed oceans, the swung pendulums
mastering prime, Schwarzschild dead at the East Front,

Moseley in Gallipoli, and De Sitter with his universe
emptied mathematically of matter in order to conjure
mass and energy in motion—our inhabited world.

Gone the ether with its airy thinness cicatrizing light,
planets, those "wild sheep," in daisy chains of epicycles
dervishing a centered earth. Newton's apple plunges

down the parallax of a rabbit hole, its wake a bend
of starlight tacking the halo of an eclipsed sun
and clocks ticking tick to the measure of every eye:

the genius's equation like a single stone launched
to shatter the foundations. So, you teach yourself tensor,
mastering scales, and limp through Aquinas' *Summa.*

So, in three years: your perpetual vows, your first Mass.
Introibo ad altare Dei. Ad Gloriam. You lift the cup—
in its shivering well the horizon of the Hidden.

(Trajectory)

I have known the dreadful dissolution, seen all
perish again and again, every atom dissolved
into the fathomless, the wild infinity, an ocean

emptied of everything. Utter darkness. Who can count
the creations that have passed away, the creations
risen afresh in the eye-blink eons of the *Puranas?*

And in this, our newest fraught iteration,
on Sobral and Príncipe, crews ready plates to catch
the moon's black coin dissolve the sun. Island hush.

Occultation. Radiant corona. Behind the blaze
arc-seconds of stars while Eddington deduces proof,
the known strata of the physical phase-shifted

to uncertainty in the slimmest bending of light.
He would play the universe—a symphony scaled
in constants, seven harmonic notes, link electron

to galaxy in the finest structures, unfathomable
as Bottom's bottomless dream, and mentored you,
his protégé, the "plump priest" with your collar

circumspect, with your speculations plumb: *I found*
M. Lemaître a very brilliant student, clear-sighted,
wonderfully quick. And you at the border of naught:

"We can think of a convex polyhedron, enclosing
all stars, all particles of which matter is formed,
the universe a bubble dipped in a sea of nothingness."

(Scope)

So let there be Shakespeare: *I have had a most rare*
vision—I have had a dream—past the wit of man
to say what dream this was: In St. Edmund's you parse

the puzzle of simultaneity where two events
accelerating uniformly in curved space veer
as Einstein believed into their relative intervals,

and one's face traveling at light speed vanishes
from the mirror before one, for nothing arrives
let alone is reflected till it gets where it's going—

and no master clock evident, no synchronous
tick, though trains leave their stations, elevators
plunge in their arrow vacuum good as standing still,

while you accelerate on your own trajectory:
Cambridge to Harvard, the Observatory's dome,
its brass eye ranging at a crest of winding stairs,

its cannonballs for bearings, Shapley charging you
to track the variables, spectra, the radial velocities:
MIT, Dominion, Lowell, Mount Wilson, each scope

opening the gathering vistas of nuance and error—
as though the painted desert you witness with Slipher,
its bends and colors, its outsized beauty and scale,

were the bright figure of your incipient sublime,
by datum to datum mastering the farthest fields,
one grain accomplishing vastness in a torrid noon.

(Vector)

In a life below decks in a great ship, windowless,
butterflies in lamplight are moving as they move.
Fish swim indifferently inside their bowl, two men

toss a ball, each to each, as the ship speeds, head-
long ahead, and nothing's driven back to the stern
since to go with this motion is to be moored in port.

From the tallest mountain at the mind's white pole
a cannon fires its charges into space, progressive
speed, till one ball, by falling, flies, by flying, falls.

Now the surfer catches a wave of frozen light
and rides it motionless to an impossible shore
where he reckons sand the particles of his path—

and twins, one traveled from earthbound earth,
the other staying home, meet again after years,
each to the other younger from when he left.

The cat in its dire box keeps equally live and dead,
the poison released, should hammer shatter flask
when the atom decays, which it may not, or it may.

You, who chose two ways equally at once, circuit
the conferences, meetings fueled by enigma,
mixing with the eminent and their sidereal regard,

your morning Masses before library and lab.
All outcomes must be possible in the system—Schrödinger.
In your life's chosen box, this con-celebration.

(Proscenium)

"We can compare space-time to an open, conic cup…"
at bottom: the first instant, the now with no before.
Or say galaxies are dots on a balloon's inflating skin,

the telescope a time machine, the past an aperture,
our looking out, away, a way of looking back.
It's not what he had hoped to hear, the maestro

of the Patent Office, the machine maker's son
who had undone every absolute and wanted still
a universe like a glass sphere balancing on a pin.

And so, at Solvay, you approach him in the park.
You, with your "dog-collar," face the genius' rebuff:
Your calculations are correct, your physics abominable.

But how then explain the Dog Star's parallax,
geometries of curved space, its broken symmetry,
the brightly fleeting spectra of Kant's island worlds?

At the Metropole, dignitaries back from talks
haunt smoking room and club. Emergent autumn
with its hints of rust, brightness hurtling to the brink.

You walk the winding pathways of the Leopold
noting gardens dying back, the rare, un-leafing trees,
mallards on Maalbeek pond mirrored with sky,

that rose-ringed parakeet on its branch, errant
from the habitat of its origin and still at home:
"There are two paths to truth; I have chosen both."

(Observance)
Edwin Hubble

"Tall, strong, beautiful, with the shoulders of Hermes
of Praxiteles, that is how my wife first fashioned me,
I who proved our Milky Way but another galaxy

among the *Nebelflecken* fleeing breakneck with the rest
by the law, the constant, the time that bear my name:
Hubble, stamped with Newton, Copernicus, Galileo.

Not bad for an Ozark farm boy hodded off to Oxford
on a Rhodes, who tailored himself to tweeds and speaks
the King's English, as though he'd suckled on shires.

Astronomy, I attest, is a history of receding horizons,
though mine tend to open to dinners with Stravinsky,
the Fairbanks, and *coup de maître*, my surprise star-turn

at the Oscars: spotlights, applause, the whole heavens
blue-shifted to me. Still—nothing headier than nights
on Mt. Wilson, eye at the lens, my briar pipe glowing,

Humason at the spectrascope tracing the light shifts
who was my mule driver. His habits—straight poker,
panther juice—try the soul, but he's brilliant at the shot.

Odd, too, the little priest who came to visit years ago,
that he should account for nebulas' radial velocities
two years before me, though I only trust the data—

how he looked calmly pleased at Einstein's recantation:
The most beautiful solution to creation I have ever heard.
So clocks reel back with space—camera, action, light."

(Shore)

Along the dune-sidled folds of the *plage*, the waves
roil imperturbably their endless perturbations:
Der Haan, West Flanders. Where in legend a rooster

crowed to save the drowning in a wreck offshore.
Where in *la belle époque* kings came to gab and golf.
Where, now, you visit the genius, exiled with his family,

for whom Germany has become death, the warrant
signed by the new Führer—calls to kill the pacifist
whose cosmos is brainchild of "The Eternal Jew."

The military system is the worst outcrop of herd nature,
your new friend will write, and *I hold pure thought*
a great reality as the ancients dreamed—on this shore

contemplating the field, or practicing the violin.
Now, as at the Athenaeum, you roll a cigarette,
peeling apart your own to replenish his store

while bodyguards walk behind. *It was the experience*
of mystery—even mixed with fear—that engendered
religion, the existence of something we cannot penetrate.

But in that thought: nature's reason alone, the eternity
of this world, alone, its marvelous structure, no God,
and life beyond death the absurd desire of feeble souls.

And you? "In the face of suffering, we must drop books
and pray." Nothing crows from the dunes. The sea,
the seething littoral, churns for its night of broken glass.

The Death of One God Is the Death of All

I believe in Spinoza's God who reveals himself in the harmony of all that exists, but not in a God who concerns himself with the fate and actions of human beings.

ALBERT EINSTEIN

(Melisma)

One note, another, in the parlor's angled light:
your fingers flaring across keys, the waiting clavier,
its felt hammers striking strings, resonant frequency

borne from score to bridge to sounding board,
coupling every gradient of energy into air.
So your moments fill with the shapeliness of song

here in the safe flat beside the Town Hall, its façade
a medieval choreography of burghers, saints,
secular cathedral, while the Reich's page turners

goose-step through your streets. You saw, advancing,
this second coming, the library at Louvain again
a torched sanctum, melted webs of steel, charred cocoon.

You'd have made your way to the coast, Pas-de-Calais,
and over the channel, father, mother in tow,
would have beaten to the pass the panzers at Dunkirk

that turned you back and locked you in retreat.
In Princeton Einstein has written his letter, his fear
of atoms concerted to bombs by German hands,

the President in seclusion committing the secret funds.
Now this bright November sun of Berchtesgaden,
the neutral king portioning his pact with Hitler.

Is there a providence at the heart of quantum chance,
the risk of the Pianist whose score evolves the keys?
Point and purpose hazarded on scales across scales.

(Calculus)

Now in earshot of you—the scale that shatters scales:
50 freight cars x 50 per car x 1.5 trains per day
x 1066 days = 4,000,000 Jews "resettled to the East"

exclusive of the death squads, and each one eclipsed
behind the death gate's limit, its prevailing West,
and Himmler petitioning the Minister of Transport

"I must have more trains": among them cattle cars
out of Brussels, out of Antwerp via Breendonk
and Malines—your seminary within hailing distance

of the moated barracks where Öbersturmführer Asche
assembles them for Auschwitz, Birkenau, Bergen-Belsen:
Asche to ash along the sideline track through Louvain.

That fall afternoon, your father collapses on a tram
and the one who sits beside him wears a yellow star.
We have the duty of conscience to strive for resistance

declares His Holiness van Roey. And you, good son
charged to attend your mother, leaven act with prayer
like an untestable theorem, listening into the vacuum.

But to see the singularity in a sphere composed of dust,
to see beyond the given limit to the horizon where light
plunges permanently into the void: your "dust solution"

by which space and time contract to nil—how to reconcile
the math when the metaphor waxes real, gravity, graves,
cinder clouds, a calculus of stars red shifting on the rails?

(Chamber)

Sunflower plumage, a pulsing body alive with song:
the Pope's canary, perched ex cathedra on his shoulder,
sings nothing of what is past, or passing, or to come.

Gretchen, his favorite, freed from her cage, keeps vigil
there, while Pius, rail-thin, pallid as a plaster saint,
eats alone according to his habit, the staunch observance

of his solitude, that lifted gaze for which he is revered.
Scholar, classicist, holy man, bureaucrat, former nuncio
to the Reich, invoker of conclaves and concordats:

should he speak the word that utters condemnation
to the bestial, the antichrist? And him the Vicar of Christ
caught in the inertia of his prudence, his well-meant

action at a distance that would preserve his own tribe,
or risk the fury, martyrdom, His Church a shambles?
The laws which bind civilized people together

have been violated, he broadcasts on Christmas,
his rhetoric a dark wood veiling Buchenwald,
the telegrams to Hitler, his silence at the roundups

near Vatican walls: culpability caught by hindsight,
the encyclical denouncing hate shelved for diplomacy.
In the photograph you look up at him, your pontiff,

as he welcomes you, obedient, open, to his throne.
And had *he* donned the yellow star? History's "What if."
O golden haired Margaret, O ashen haired Shulamith.

(Aperture)

And so, let the mind commit a thought experiment,
split the physicist from priest like a single photon
shot through a screen, charting the divergent paths:

—"Consider a civilization where music is unknown,
only acoustics and frequencies, the notes like an air
un-breathable for the animal in its element.

Is this not where our method leads us, into matter
as matter, force as force, the amplitudes a blank smoke
unnecessary—number as number and nothing more?"

—"Infinity is such an artistic creation, all symmetry
and elegance, but your method smacks of metaphysics,
lifeless life, and the Bible is not a textbook of science.

If relativity theory had been necessary to salvation
it would have been revealed to St. Paul or Moses.
Still, the deeper we penetrate the universal mystery

the more we will find one law and one goodness."
—"Newton's *Principia*, Abbe Mendel and his peas,
from quantum to quanta—all purposeless process."

—"Time's arrow at t=o has a barb at each end
that makes the infinite universe a buried corpse.
Our world is now a world where something happens,

with the world's matter present from the beginning,
with the world's story to be written step by step."
—"In venom, crematoria, the animal's voided blood."

(Tenebrae)

This shadowgraph performance of familiar life, shadow
of an elbow on a shadow table, the shadow ink flowing
over shadow paper, the body no more than a spectral

orchestration, specks whirling with specks in a greater
emptiness, within, without, the fragile, mutable matter
of ourselves, flotsam from the quantum sea, emergent,

or devolved from some more perfect symmetry, broken
into world-lines and geodesics, cathedral-webs of space,
and time, statistical magician, pulls a rabbit from its hat: us.

God does not play dice with the universe, but where is
Der Alte when you need Him? Newton's Divine Observer
letting each passing, solitary, sum-over-history break

on Him, with our local sufferings, astride the non-local:
the solving, unsatisfying, tunneling path of letting it happen?
So, on the mesa, the Sangre de Cristo a roiling geometry

of light and shade, the Lord Rapid Rupture assembles
the luminaries, subcritical mass to critical mass,
to ensure the Bomb's tamper attains maximal efficiency.

And you, forgotten in your shadow-life in the outskirts
of Hell, consider the passage you struck years before:
"I think that everyone who believes in a supreme being

supporting every life, every action, believes that God
is essentially hidden, and may be glad also to see
how present physics provides a veil hiding the creation."

(Sanctum)

Darkness on the face of the deep, darkness hidden
by darkness, no time before time, before existence
and non-existence, but to climb as the mystic said

to the high mountains, where there is no shadow,
only sun. So in mind you reverse the symmetry
to walk beside him in Gröenendael, green valley,

with his tablet and stylus to the Soignes' axel tree
where clarity shines with the exactness of equations,
his soul become a live coal in the fire of infinite love

by which he sees through the multiplicity of things:
*To know it we must be in it, beyond the mind, above
our created being, in that Eternal Point where all*

*our lines begin and end, where they lose their name,
become that very One the Point is, and yet remain
themselves nought else but lines that come to an end.*

To give, then, image to the Imageless, for in depths
of the Real there is no ground, only fathomless sea,
life fashioned on the bedrock of the empty Abyss:

there, where the Source ceaselessly begets, un-begotten,
there, where the Love between breathes out and flows,
there, where the Mirror sees itself, Life-Giving-Life,

while light in its nakedness penetrates air, a plenitude,
like the dusk sky descended perfectly inside a cove,
the mind, now, observing, unguarded and un-walled.

(Imago)

But to discern God's will in this will o' the wisp world,
the seeming random daubs conjuring a picture whole,
ice melting, magnetism from dead metal, and time itself

a shatter of moments, phase shifted, from the everlasting
into these vectors of growth and decay: flatlanders aware,
unaware, endowed with a prized biological contraption

whereby they know *Nature does not act by purposes*,
that *Nature in itself has no reverence for life*.
And in your notebooks with the neat calculations,

graphs, your parsing of uncertainty, elliptical space,
those passages translated from Ruysbroeck's *Tabernacle:*
la lumière éternelle engloutissant toutes...une chaleur mystérieuse.

Shall we call it God's non-locality, every where at once,
that the eye altering the measure of light, this chamber eye,
misses, calibrated as it is for predator and prey.

Human being is an animal, you wrote, and human being
is a child of God: while in the animal world the transports
gain frequency, annihilated cargo, in this goldilocks world

with all the dials set for our arrival—luck like grace,
and Love like gravitation, a force, so the saint dreamed,
attracting the scattered sparks, jumbled puzzle, to Itself.

So, in your house, with friends you gather again to pray:
"Transcendence isn't passage; it's adding one life to another."
Light drawn to light in the image of every victim's face.

(Repertory)

The processional enters with its deliberate masques:
eight thousand generations, more or less, of diligent pain.
Though tonight in the theater it is Molière, *Le Misanthrope,*

where the baseness of the species finds self-reproach.
You sit in the dark before the bright-lit proscenium
while outside, all around you, it is *Faust* playing out

without its second part to redeem the striving soul:
the flag, demonic, rippling in the public square, threats,
colleagues taken for forced labor, taken to the camps.

And you accused of being friends with Jews, the rector
seized for refusing to give the student names, the Jew,
Jesus, nailed again to the pattern of a crooked cross.

Enter Alceste: *That I could break with the human race.*
Do you follow back the drama to its first unfolding,
Australopithecus, Homo habilis, Home erectus, African Eve:

an original sin that's wired and woven, mitochondrial,
into the flesh, forgotten genocides, the dead ends,
along the long out-branching long ago of what we are?

Your mother in her seat shifts intently at your side.
Ascent? Descent? Encoded hate. Passivity. The guilt of it.
And the days ahead of discipline, prayer, the soul's work

of holding itself true—*forma omnium, materia omnium,*
essentia omnium, omnia sunt in ipsa divina essentia:
Everything that is, is in the very essence of God.

(Signature)

And the music of what happens? Hiss and battle strafe,
the flocks in rhythm over blood sluice and gas chamber.
In my father's house are many mansions. Thus, in depths

of the rabbit hole you glimpse a flickering strobe:
Chance? Freedom? Divine life emptied into conditions,
dispossessed among the dispossessed, the dispossessing.

Thus: "God is hidden, hidden, even, from the beginning
of creation." Thus, too: what you called "the strangeness
of the universe," and relativity "a purely scientific matter

neither theistic nor atheistic, nothing whatsoever to do
with religion." To consider, then, the black body problem
where all light absorbed renders the object invisible:

or consciousness, as Schrödinger mused, liberated
from time by physical theory, and indestructible, our
senses unaccountable by the mind that requires them:

It resides upon them, is pieced together from them,
yet the mind cannot really be said to contain them.
While in the vacuum's zero all possible wavelengths

exist until they dazzle into tune and what is played
is played—a symphony, an open role of the dice:
as now the bombers veer overhead, and your house

explodes around you, you alive in the mangled room.
Miracle? Ananke's chosen? Probability's favored child?
A God of the gulf, engulfing, not born of the gaps.

(Veil)
Robert Oppenheimer

"When they christened me secretly Rapid Rupture
I recalled the code my father taught me, *Deed before Creed*,
my aim to ensure the weapon as soon as prudent

but separating the isotope proved most impractical.
So, we shifted from gun-type to a concerted design
that allowed the device to detonate by implosion.

We called it 'the Christy gadget,' after my student
who mapped the initiator for the chain reaction.
When Groves approved the test, our congregation

made its way to Ground Zero, not far from Pope:
White Sands, the range a kind of theater in the round,
lushly barren, sky blue as in a painting by Magritte.

At first, I thought to place the weapon in its vessel,
spherical chalice, for containment, then opted to raise
the steel cup above to test the power. You know

what followed, though I'll quote again the Gita's lines:
If the radiance of a thousand suns were to burst at once
into the sky, it would be like the splendor of the Mighty One.

And after: desert burned to a green glass, Vishnu
transfigured in a version of Tabor—*I have become Death,*
shatterer of worlds, the clouds parting over Nagasaki.

I named the site Trinity to honor my old lover,
a suicide, its name from one of Donne's *Holy Sonnets*:
how the great artist separates light from darkness...."

(Fractal)

And after the end the pat outbreak of rapture, the gone
taken into accountable absence, unaccountably vast:
the light years in atoms, the hair's breadth between stars.

Or picture a force newly rippling the vacuum, a field
risen like a violin's tuned strings, its harmonics and tones,
while outside the metal world every wave still exists

undetectable: metaphor for the dead, or for the living?
In city squares the crowds are rejoicing, the air infused
with summer's consequent light. You photograph them

as you photographed your room's obliterated walls,
will photograph your travels to Cape Town, Assisi,
in the world you'll know after a world's destroyed—

light through a shutter, paper, emulsion, the imprint
of time. To picture God's eye that singular camera,
or to picture four dimensions an infinite Now, ever-

lasting, forever complete and forever in passage,
a hologram splintered, fractal, the whole in each part.
In my father's house, He said, *are many mansions.*

Mansions in a house, as though the part happened
to out-build the whole? Let it be Brussels, 1945,
your innocuous apartment on the Rue de Braekeleer.

You sit in the sitting room reading your Ruysbroeck.
then turn to your piano, the one beloved and saved,
dusk through blinds, your fingers ranging the scales.

Of Motion, the Ever-Brightening Origin

What is man in nature? A nothing compared to the infinite, a whole compared to the nothing, a middle point between all and nothing, infinitely remote from any understanding of the extremes; the end of things and their principles are unattainably hidden from him in impenetrable secrecy....What can he do, then, but perceive some semblance of the middle of things, eternally hopeless of knowing either their principles or their end? All things come out of nothing and are carried onwards to infinity.

PASCAL

(Stream)

Jubilant billowing from the choir loft, throngs in song,
the faithful processing through the chapel's threshold,
bearing with them the statue, image of the apparition:

the sun dancing in its window in the clouds, the sun
a burning halo raining petals, in the center of its seal
Joseph with infant Jesus, around them daylight stars.

"How can one avoid being skeptical, Coimbra seeing
nothing of the witness, of the events at Fatima?"
You, caught in the crosshairs of your paths to truth:

piety and feasts, statistical notions, Masses and mass,
and energy immanent *in Galilean local coordinates*
while the universe speeds its breakneck transcendence,

the galaxies sanctuaries in recession without end.
So, you saw lambda on the right hand not the left,
Einstein's crystalline sphere in pin-point balance

tipped from the equation: "The cosmological constant
may be compared to iron rods hidden inside a building,
indispensible to the structure of a synthesis more vast."

Saw photons decoupled into light in an instant's surge.
Saw horizons cooling and calibrated out of the fog.
Saw, before Oppenheimer, stars in radial collapse,

him leaving you uncited. And the Princeton letter
with the master's judgment: *I am unable to believe
that such an ugly thing should be realized in nature.*

(Nexus)

To you even so comes the open door: to commune
with Einstein, Gödel, Bohr: and, so, to enter life
inside the magic circle, its vivid talk, your star again

in ascent, though the good son sadly begs to decline,
that future eclipsed behind the orbit of your duty.
Turn, then, to Pascal's double infinity, infinite depth,

infinite immensity, and nature a Janus face of cold
extremes, vast extents, where mind drifts uncertainly,
and everything seen *an imperceptible dot* stretched

above *the greater nothingness beyond our reach—*
seeing in him your shadow double, mathematician,
priest, drawn by both to the *astonishing processes.*

Observe: to derive a solution to the problem of three
bodies, in space or scalar field, how the perturbation
of one in motion with the other is caused by the third.

Observe: geometry at the quantum level is nonlocal,
the Planck threshold a phase from which spacetime
emerges, before which no space no time, nowhere.

Observe: Contrary to Pascal, one cannot deduce God
from infinite nature. Better to prefer *deus absconditus,*
God supremely inaccessible, hidden, unknowable.

But from the Unknowable, the known and its motion,
all in concert. *These extremes touch and join by going
in opposite directions, and meet in God, in God alone.*

(Contratemps)

All one, one would believe, and *Behind Every Door,*
God: The Pope in his prayerful speech bearing witness
to the august instant of the primordial Fiat Lux,

confirmation of the contingent universe from the hands
of the creator, well founded deduction, a bursting forth
from nothing into a sea of light, gesture of generous love.

Never, it appears, will you live it down, Pius's piety
the confirming gaffe, your "two paths" confused,
and you returned from Rome, bruising into class,

unlike (students noted) your irrepressibly cheerful self—
by your lights the primordial atom still unproven,
curtailed, perhaps, by an earlier stage of contraction

unaccounted for as yet in all empirical data, in all
the exacting equations clarifying a lens on the known:
the phoenix universe you entertained, "very beautiful."

Or the fact when wave functions collapse, it's the eye
parsing the probable into the real, extemporizing all
possible outcomes, many worlds, the real it turns out

more prodigal than Pascal's infinities, finitudes rolling
just beyond the glass edges of science and faith
in the bottoming abyss below before, now, and after

in which, in your time, you labor behind the scenes
to salvage the truth, its necessity, its separateness:
the fraught word of telling your infallible pope no.

(Agnus)
George Gamow

"Mary had little lambda. His fleece was Jesus—Ha!
Of course, back in Odessa as child, I had to discover
for myself, so I take communion in Orthodox Church,

run home with bread and wine secreted in my cheek,
place it under microscope—I see no transubstantiation.
That's experiment that made me, Gamow, scientist.

Can you imagine, from hocus pocus to nucleosynthesis,
how in first five minutes, light, dense particle soup,
recombines to form self, then bridges unbridgeable path

to make hydrogen, helium, all our heavier elements
without which no inflation, so no so-called Big Bang
since priest could not account for equal values: stretch

of cosmic rays across scope of universe from this mix
I call *ylem*, from Middle English word for substance.
When Pope says this or Pope says that I have great fun,

add chunks of speech to my papers, watch eyebrows
rise, not God. But priest is excellent, better with math
than me, I admit, though he still believes in fairy tales.

It took atheist to see what must remain at radio end
of spectrum, and how his swelling lambda came to be,
I who with my wife once braved Black Sea in kayak

to escape Soviet Union—failure. How I'll never forget
sight of this dolphin I glimpsed through passing wave
illuminated, just then, by sun sinking below horizon."

(Anthropic)

This process of coming to life: autocatalysis of wave
to particle, particle to wave, from indeterminacy,
such that the photons fuse, the sun shines, the clay,

crystalline in its shallow pool, flickers into motion
so that in time the observer might observe, so that
in mind's conjuring what had come to be must be

brought before the mind as though it had not been,
could not be, until fashioned from the probabilities:
and all that might have been, too, fanning out deeply.

The theory says a lot, but does not really bring us any closer
to the secret of des Alten, the Old One, so Einstein
confided to Born. And now the master's dead is he

gifted with the Old One's secret, and your mother,
the windows of both their faces shaded and shut?
All goes onward and outward, nothing collapses—Whitman:

except the wave function out of its eternal now
below the proton's spin, before Planck's length waxes
from nothing, and nothing there until it's measured—

who measures the dead? *For our perpetual vows*
Canon Lemaître designed a brilliant course, how the life
of the mind carries the image of a nebula expanding,

spirit formed in contact with matter, the world-lines
of our becoming a further transcendence promising
what follows. Pure miracle? No. A phase. A threshold.

(Cinema)

In the film that doesn't begin and never ends, a man
wakes, drives to a country farmhouse where he finds
the guests he knows from his recurring dream, each

telling their own strange tale to him, the architect
called in to pitch his new design—a fratricidal son,
that ventriloquist whose dummy mouths his life–

progressive horror, till from his nightmare the man
wakes, drives to a country farmhouse where he finds
the guests he knows from his recurring dream....

So, with *Dead of Night*, Bondi, Gold, and Hoyle wake
to their design, the universe a Steady State, a cloud
that never moves from its mountaintop, one droplet

added for every one lost. Or like our own bodies
freshened cell by cell, creation continuous, God-less,
and atoms bred from atoms from alchemical stars.

You drive with Hoyle in the hills above Montalcino,
the cloth merchant's son, outspoken, caustic, truant,
who would label you comically "The Big Bang Man,"

arguing the probabilities: "What matter, Fred, creates
itself?" "Nothing, my dear Georges, then in an instant
a universe?" All that is, is, is spinning on a pencil point.

And you in his dinner portrait of you, a Friday fast,
coveting his steak, the enormous, undesired fish
appearing to stay the same size however much you eat.

(Spiritus)

Stylus, number wheel, gear tooth, cog, a falling weight
accomplishes the carry: so, the years add up, interlocked,
as on a Pascaline to you at your Burroughs, desk-sized,

its circuits and sequences programmed with your code:
celestial mechanics as your students crowd the bulk,
nebulae cast in binaries coalescing from the expanse,

and the calibrated universe shaped as by an algorithm,
the way crystal calculates to crystal, self-generating,
ramified in solution, salt, pattern, Adamic brick and clay.

Let it be, then, Ruysbroeck's *sparkling stone*, emergent
in matter's ontogeny, a seeded cascade into sentience,
the code in us that shows, you believed, "the universe

is not out of reach...this is Eden, garden that grows
so that it might see." Let it be Newton's miracle pin
balanced on its mirror, the possible impossibility: be

the emptying, first flash like foxfire quickened out
of Nil, catalytic light unfurling into net—galaxies,
planets—where the iterative urge burgeons into soul,

pebble on which its new name will be written, the holy
contracted into panoply, an extrication, the risk
of immanence: dewdrop pendant on a grass blade, the

suffering one forsaken on his deliberate tree. And you
in your *jouissance* parsing assemblers, your *Hoc est Corpus*
at the Mass, the *riffraff* in the *ylem* winnowing up.

(Corpus)

For all of it, how presumptuous, we thinking reeds,
unable as we are to stand outside the human, the cost
of our becoming, all becoming, a ripple of sun across

the leopard's back as it locks on the gazelle, prodigal
orders of blood and contingency, signifying nothing.
Or, if not, a hidden sum in the corpus of the random.

Each evening, after class, out with the student throng,
you carry, boisterous, your conversations to the cafés,
take your meals at the Majestic, comfortable routine.

And when the violence comes, like a recessive flaw
in the source code of history, the binaries—Flemish,
Walloon—shatter again your safe sphere with bricks

through your windows for having counseled peace.
Cape Town, Chicago, Berkeley, Milan, Rome—unreal
the life passing, and you ready with your camera

limning the moment, taking its measure, gradations
of light and shade, companions, vistas, incalculable
the event horizon of the present arrowing on ahead

and tied to a promise, Augustine knew, by memory:
that time, Paris, your trip to program the new machine,
hours at it, and afterwards till almost dawn your beers

with friends, you in your soutane walking wryly past
the flagrant women, the Moulin Rouge, your big laugh
explosive in the lobby: "We have been to the Pigalle!"

(Canto)

Is it motion itself that makes the day? Or is it the time
taken by that motion? Or is it both? the saint asked,
searchingly—*Deus creator omnium*: the measure

of mind made by the Maker of minds, and time
come to existence only observable as time, phase
transition to the radio spectrum, pre-recombinant,

the primordial light unchanged from the initial
sea of light, a television hiss homing everywhere,
mysterious, incessant: as to this twenty-foot horn

where the pigeons have posited their nest, where
their white dielectric material seems the source.
And Penzias, son of Polish Jews, born the day

the Gestapo formed, his father a janitor stoking
furnaces in the Bronx, scrubs the antenna clean,
again, adjusts the cold load grounding the array.

And knows what he hears is light's first word
through time's wall, un-walled. And you, the priest
who foreknew it, envisioned this omnipresence

equation after equation, recline a little easier
into your death bed at the news, the diminuendo
never ending, the under-melody of a symphony

distantly keyed, like the tune the saint heard, *prior*
to origin, since a song is not given form to become sound,
but sound given form to become song: You enter the song.

(Matins)
Georges Lemaître

"*Mon ami, mon frère,* in the trenches nearly *mon semblable,*
Georges et Georges, though you changed back to *Joris*
to claim outright your Flemish past, a Flemish future,

let this be my last letter to you if only in my mind.
Into every horizon brims the ancient light one hears
like a primal score, before which everything evolves.

To think then of the infinite lives, each entangled,
like yours and mine, never to be separated despite,
Van Severen, the severances passing: us at the front

with our Bibles, our Bloy, his passion for the poor,
for justice, you with your felt wrongs, your drive
for redress by which you fashioned your visionary

gleam, self cult, the Fascist idol for which you died.
I preferred my silent retreats, my Poincaré, the dual
certitude of a double path, divergent, to the Truth.

Still, I pray I might have turned you from that road,
a tragic strut, your bit part on time's proscenium.
I have had my journey, too, and have followed it

faithfully, a rightness, like the eclipse I witnessed
before my own came on: the observatory in Milan,
that halo when the three bodies perfectly aligned,

not only in equations but in flesh. We are all strayed
lines in an infinite story we see, at best, darkly.
The rooster crows and thinks it makes the sun rise."

(Cove)

Sometimes it's no different than the sound of the surf,
this key of light breaking on the shore of everything,
whisper conjured out of vacuum and hush, fathomless.

On the night you died the waves were lifting, the sands
a shifting membrane at Gravelines, Calais, the North Sea
one sea, and the sands multiplying myriad after myriad

falling short of infinity. So, make each grain a universe,
each universe an origin that billows into next and next,
while each in its time, in its merciless time, waxes old

like a garment, and hastens out of sight. Now, this now,
a white heron stands at water's edge beside the inlet,
and those gathered on the walk, on the beach, pass by

un-regarding, private orbits of need and happenstance
coming to be, gathering in patterns, windfalls of seeds
along the jigsaw of a jetty—rockroses in the cracks,

delicate blooms. And of that other Now, measureless,
below the threshold of every knowing? "The evolution
of Providence," you said, "does not exclude the physical,

this living world with its random mutations, its accidence
harboring toward a goal." Is it risen, or descended,
this manifold mirror of bay and sky, horizon-less,

utterly still, utterly in motion, held, stretching across,
offered like a cup? A lifting, unencumbered, of wings.
At dawn a blood-red host; a blood-red host at nightfall.

...and the universe nothing more than dream—
and we, blind as book lice, cross the slight

horizon of a page, to miss the moment
in our desperate flittering, the Word unread,

sustaining, beneath us: purpose and path,
ash to amethyst, moth wing, seraph, breath...

TWO

This Broken Symmetry

It is because it can be loved by us, it is because it is beautiful, that the universe is a country. It is our only country here below.... We have a heavenly country but, in a sense, it is too difficult to love, because we do not know it...

SIMONE WEIL

"This Broken Symmetry" takes its occasion from the life of French phi-
losopher, mystic, and social justice advocate Simone Weil (1909-1943).
Simone Weil died of heart failure after a diagnosis of tuberculosis,
though years of ascetic practice withholding food, which many regard
her self-starvation, likely contributed to her frailty. Her brother André
Weil (1906-1998) was one of the greatest and most influential mathe-
maticians of the twentieth century. Symmetry breaking happens when
minute fluctuations acting on a system cross a critical boundary and
decide the system's future. From a hypothetical vantage outside, the
choice appears arbitrary. The universe we inhabit came into being at
the Big Bang through the breaking of its initial primordial symmetry.

The Bread of Time to Come

Time as it flows wears down and destroys that which is temporal. Accordingly, there is more eternity in the past than in the present.... Thus, the past presents us with something which is at the same time real and better than ourselves, something which can draw us upwards—a thing the future never does.

SIMONE WEIL

(Bybrook)

She adored sunsets, and her last was a flaming host
placed gravely on the ocean's tongue, indistinguishable
from dawn, the vagrant star, the soul's final morsel.

No longer now the wasted figure, self-starved, the sky
spread above the ceiling above the bed the huge refuge,
as though this plot had always been, would always be

her portion, and all the vastness nascent in that fold
flowering emptily: "I am a badly cut off piece of God."
A wind blowing east across the Channel to Gravelines

stirs the border of native trees, stirs them classically.
Their limbs broadcast nothing of the ancient news.
Their bodies bend, pliant, with each prevailing sway.

"Let the universe be to my hand a blind man's stick,
another body to my soul, my death no importance…
I am the color of dead leaves, an unnoticed insect."

Now, above her hollow in earth, a few friends circle,
then kneel, where in time a belated stone will rest,
where they pray now, where now one throws a bouquet

to crest the plain wood box, and her slenderest stem
cut that fixed her to her waiting: while the summoned
priest, un-showing, turns back from his mistaken train

through crowds, numb, that in time will be new crowds
to settle beyond the trees in queues for Cinema World.
How grandly fleet the light in each commodious cave.

(Roots)

He is waiting at the door of "Miss Simone," curled there
as though in utero—the boy she tutors, his new words
copied daily in a notebook, his future's hampered code.

She likes her room at the top of the cottage, stars at night,
the branches full of birds, having been denied her wish
to be smuggled into France, air dropped, to die a sacrifice,

not withering away in the Ministry Offices editing tracts,
composing her *Need for Roots*, de Gaulle thinking her mad,
and in her notebook, her last texts: "As in Christ's parable,

I am that fig tree, barren." Or any stone on which seed falls,
never to be fleshed. But to partake of the Communion,
the sacrament an image, perfect, of the universe entire,

the meal that she denies herself, unlike those few evenings
here in Notting Hill, before the nightly migraines wake her—
her landlady's warm offerings of coffee and buttered bread.

Not long now until the sanitarium in Ashford, her lungs
wasting, she refusing food to ally her soul with the starving
at home, the world uprooted, herself the frailest cutting

from the Hidden: "God is not in time. We are abandoned.
But only from the past, absolutely beyond our reach, real,
only from the past alone will renewal come, if we love it."

Let it be Villanueva, ten years before, at seaside. She lives
in her bathing suit, not dressing for meals, her rags dropped,
her skin wet. And a fisherman threads a flower in her hair.

(Decreation)

But to enter the uncreated, Nothing's naked open sea,
before God abandoned God to these various forms
of hunger, gravity riveted plumb in every scattered part,

and each flung *I* like a standing pole to blot the infinite,
as if creation at its root were rooted in cross-purposes:
"My great desire is to lose all will, lose all personal being."

What at best is God but a beggar in this world emergent
as when an ocean recedes into itself and shores appear,
never once again but for the first time, a slough, a seething,

but in the self's self-possessed imagining of a universe
beyond which, in emptiness, the beggar whispers secretly
self's self-renouncing song, for "only God can love God."

Yet in this broken symmetry our love, she said, should stretch
across all of space, spread equally in every portion of it:
so how does it manifest, this knowing of beauty, of bridges—

all things *metaxu,* metaphors, to lead us out, and even evil
a form of mercy: this world at once "the barrier, the closed
door, and the way through" from one to another and then

to God. And this passing fictive I, born to really die, to be
but a little pile of brute matter, how does it become "the bird
with golden wings that pierces through the egg of the world?"

It must wait like Electra for the dead Orestes to return,
like Christ in Gethsemane, God waiting in God's absence
like a beggar, God waiting for God under the olive trees.

(Riverside)
André Weil

"Below the brownstone-solid bulwark of the Palisades,
flowing and flown, this river appears a living manifold,
infinitely transmutable, congruent to us only by its will.

My sister watches, it seems, for hours from our window
as if she saw another window open to, maybe beyond
the scene, a vision captivating but foreign to everything.

When we were young during the War, we'd hike a hill
to that summer house in the Alps above our lone resort,
the garden grown half-wild with its panoply of blooms,

and the mountains snow-covered against the bluest sky,
like something from Friedrich—her laughter at our reciting
Cyrano together, her obstinacy at the prospect of leaving:

indomitable Simone—how do I save her from herself?
Sundays she goes to Mass at Corpus Christi, and again
to worship at that church in Harlem, loving as she does

the singing and shouting, the joyous dancing in the aisles—
she who drabs herself in breeches and refuses baptism.
But, still, she nestles my newborn, Sylvie—her 'Patapon'—

in her arms, and tells Eveline the child should be baptized:
daughter of agnostic Jews whose faith her aunt refuses,
her counsel practical, regardless of what faith, or none,

the child comes to choose. I take mine, if any, from Arjuna:
I see you everywhere, Lord of the Universe—faces, bellies, arms, eyes,
I see you, Manifold One, who have no beginning, no middle, no end."

(Font)

New York bound, a reek of diesel from its pluming stacks,
the *Serpa-Pinto* churns ahead through weeks of rolling swells,
in its hold a cache of refugees, in its cabins the affluent—

all escapees in passage from the muzzle of naked force.
Sickened from her lower berth, she stretches out on deck,
daughter of the Chosen who has chosen contumacy.

Here, in a middle vastness, with other "wretched mortals"
pressing themselves to the rail, wordless as in a desert,
will this be the evening all suddenly refracts and shines?

"What could be more beautiful than the fugitive folds
of waves, the near eternal folds of mountains? This world,
to us, is the only reality available, and we must love it

in all its terror, or love the imagined with its self-deceits…
Oh, if we are torpedoed what a beautiful baptismal font!"
She looks out into the ocean, the boat, herself, the planet,

infinitely tiny specks in an infinite web of necessity,
and matter the measure of distance to her emptied God.
Osiris, Melchizedek, Krishna, incarnations of the Word

before the Word-Made-Flesh—how can the emptied God
be with us if not in our imagining? Through a porthole
the hall mills with voyagers, father, mother, the hold below:

Like so many currents of water rushing headlong for the sea,
or like moths ablaze for the flame, so the heroes of this world,
and even the teeming worlds run to their deaths in your mouths.

(Anathema)

She only reads what she hungers for, only when she has
the appetite for it, so she reveals to her confessor,
Father Perrin, and even, then, she does not read but eats—

eats Plato, Pythagoras, eats Aeschylus and Rousseau
at that café in Vichy Marseille, her books, papers stacked
while her friend in the photo twirls his spoon in cream:

eats enough to know how from its infancy the Church
has gorged on power, *Anathema sit*, and tells the priest so,
and casts herself off with the others cast off, to remain

"with those that cannot enter, the many things God loves
because they exist, that could not exist without God's love":
eats, too, therefore, a knowledge of the chicken yard—

how other animals fall upon a wounded hen, each driven
to give pain the way pistons inflict the engine's demands,
and God's love most evident in that solitary suffering:

eats, eats until the need to consume is consumed in prayer,
her terrible prayer. "Father, Father, in Christ's name
grant me this: that my will become famished of any desire

for bodily movement, for all hope of movement. Let me be
deaf, blind, bereft—incapable wholly of all sensation,
paralytic, unable to bridge even one thought to another.

Transfigure me now, though my faith is imperfect, as if
it was perfect, in the name of Christ to the body of Christ,
grant me this, now, to be picked clean, devoured by God."

(Le Poët)

Not as in that Alpine photo below the chalet years before,
smiling into the camera's caress of light, skis edging grass
and the downhill's white rush of snow, but on the cold floor

in Le Poët (long lavender fields in autumn mountain air)
she sleeps fitfully, having refused the heartened room
where her parents rest, where she did not want to wake,

but hoped to be greeted as Plato did Diogenes, *Good Day,*
dog, as though by naming to banish the animal inside her,
as though by self-cruelty prune gravity from the terrestrial.

What she sees looking back is the species' errant slalom,
downward track of monkey mind past stations pointing up.
Ahead: decadence, opulent flat-out byway heading nowhere,

this hopelessness abiding until humans resume their caves.
Daily she digs potatoes with the locals, nightly memorizes
in its original Greek the Our Father, an "infinite sweetness"

until, with great concentration, she repeats it over and over,
its words tearing the thoughts from her body: her transport
to a place "outside space," no vantage, no point of view—

space itself opened, she would recount, filled with silence,
"a true silence, not absence of sound," like song perfected.
While in Le Poët long lavender fields in autumn mountain air

brim in quickening chill, so on the church the sundial brims
along its raised Vitruvian arms and the script's gilded light
beyond all longing not to be: *Look Into My Living Heart, See Life.*

(Harvest)
Gustave Thibon

"Like someone who has spent long hours among the vines,
prematurely old, bent, that's how she looked to me that day
we met in Avignon, who hadn't picked yet a single cluster,

her face wan, faded like a fresco angel in the Palais des Papes.
Only her eyes, magnificent, only her eyes alone triumphed
in that shipwreck of beauty, with their look of something

foreign to this world. She refused our room in Saint-Marcel,
chose the ruin, earthen-floored beside the wood, its scatter
of rat *merde*, its pine needle mattress and peasant's hearth,

that one small window from which she'd view the Rhone—
her 'fairy tale house,' she'd say, 'rest, fresh fruit, delicious air,'
the fear she felt of losing herself among sensual pleasures.

One time I found her sitting, still, on the tree trunk in front,
lost in contemplation, and sensed just then a correspondence—
the beauty of that soul and the landscape's tender majesty.

But, how raw, her friends suffered her will for immolation,
she who chided me for withholding my true measure
of stripping myself away. For her, the beauty of the world

was the mouth of a labyrinth: in the center, there God waits
to eat the soul. So, in Saint Julien she joined with harvesters,
disappearing among rows of pendant grapes, embodied wine,

cutting free the perfectly nurtured bruise-colored fruit, hour
by hour, for days, her sandaled feet bleeding, purifying her
she'd say until 'I see the landscape as it is when I'm not there.'"

(Montségur)

High, high and sure, far above the poplars' spreading tips,
at the very spur's end where its lowest stones still loom
in sheer ascent, triangulate like an arrowhead, the château

holds its skull-eyed gaze heavenward: impregnable *puog*,
secure *mons*, matter's outpost, where the pure ones, *cathari*,
spirit's troubadours inside their virginal Altaforte, kept

the faith against the faithful, a consolation of the perfect,
each one an angel's genderless life trapped in the physical,
bodies bereft of goodness like all things visible, like all

created things—corrupt wastage of an evil demi-god—
the Eucharist just straw through the body's sieve, Christ
a masquerade of flesh, and impure souls fated to return

from death, their vital dross condemned to the earth—
unless, on death's bed they shun all drink, all food, until
their wine is liberated from earth, their light from the wine.

So, from Innocent's decree the armies besieged them there
in Languedoc, in Toulouse, as in Béziers and Carcassonne,
the men and women equally, equally held in God's regard,

and marched them down from the safe hill, a late Masada,
to the *prat del cremat*, cheering the screams as the flames
licked flesh, stoked pyres blanching incense to the winds

where Rome scattered coins and Neanderthals camped—
this "genius of Occitan" that set the belated Lady afire
in her own flawlessness: *a swirl upon the stair, Audiart, Audiart....*

(Marmot)

And so, for a figure of the creature consider the marmot,
clawed probing forepaws more accomplished than pickaxes
at parsing stones from earth, carting each off in its teeth,

rock pile like a mound builder's where its burrow tunnels
under, spread mat of grass at the entry, in the "living rooms"
where only one family lives, where the generations follow

there on the high meadows with the other families together
slowly expanding underground their lone itinerant systems
as one stands sentry: chatter, whistles, a warning beat of tail.

And for "this creature," her friend called her, "who was at war
with her life," who saw desire to eat, nothing but "a function
base, disgusting," consider now a marmot in hibernation,

how for months the thing curls into itself, eating nothing
and growing heavier, the body's stored, patient sustenance
like the lungs' rapt fixation on air, or heart's dimmed pulse—

life's nascent death, then a slow winnowing back into spring:
"A very fine thing to take as a model," she says, refusing
any increase in rations for years of "alimentary restrictions,"

her food gifted to Vichy camps for the enemies of Hitler.
And the marmot as marmot? A species profligate in the Alps,
on Carpathian steppes, cousin to the American prairie dog,

extinct now in the Pyrenees from the Pleistocene; dominant
females stressing competitors to miscarriage; a marmot's stored
fat believed prudent for rheumatism; every baby born blind.

(Rue de Catalan)
Selma "Mime" Weil

"Dear Monsieur, if one must be exiled one should have a view—
back home in Paris the Gardens like Earth's greenest impress
where I'd walk my children below windows of spacious flats

like our own; and here, this beach nearby the city's old port,
the Mediterranean an opulent turquoise robe unfolding itself
as ships appear to sidle off the horizon's vagrant tipping point.

Marseilles, this aged sea-metropolis buttressed by battlements
of saints, a lesser Notre Dame raised, a catafalque on its hill:
they'll come for us Jews here, too, with the operation of tigers.

André, the most reticent soldier of our fake France, ducked
firing squads. He came by boat, us shouting 'Oscar is with us'
(our code name for police), now safely left. But Simone, Simone....

As a child, once, given a gold ring, she said 'I dislike luxury,'
never liked to be kissed or played with dolls, refused to eat,
even then for the hungry. Should I be shocked years later

she would bring Trotsky to our rooms for their tête-à-tête?
Then the factory work, her barely bearing up, the going-off
to fight in Spain: we begged her to return after her wounding,

now lie about the cost for her to stay with us, safe for now,
despite the Statutory Regulations, and she to the Ministry,
'I do not know the definition of Jew': my lovely daughter,

threadbare, who regards herself one of Krishna's milkmaids,
and fathoms no kin to Palestine but hears Jesus whispering!
Dear Monsieur, if you have a daughter, pray she is not a saint."

Exceeding Music

What is the kingdom of God like? And to what shall I compare it?
    It is like a grain
of mustard seed which a man took and sowed in his garden; and it
    grew and became
a tree, and the birds of the air made nests in its branches.

LUKE, 13: 18-21

Arjuna, among all things I am the seed. There is no creature, living
    or un-living,
that would be without me.

BHAGAVAD GITA, "ELEVENTH DISCOURSE"

(Dordogne)

Yes, Ravidat, to follow the rabbit down its winding hole
below the limestone cliffs near Montignac—Périgord Noir
with its oak forests where the river flows breakneck ahead

from ancient *cluzeaux* and lookout huts clotted for refuge
against Rome, this parcel scorched for Aquitaine, its singers
accorded to war, that exceeding music, to descend again

into the whisper chamber, stone veil, womb of the species
and this time bring her with you, this scion, our secular saint,
while above the latest conqueror clamors with its cavalcade.

In this commodious cave, in the hall of bulls, aurochs rear
parietal among dun horses, a great-horned stag, its antlers
flaring like ganglia along the swelled boss—axial, synaptic—

pigments blotted, swabbed, tube-sprayed in the tallow light.
So, the galleries unfold, brede-like, in their earthen basilica,
shaft, passageway, apse and nave: rhino, bison, feline, bear…

There, among the graven lattices and symbols, a thousand
thousand overlapping and entangled, there in the darkness
where the first imaginers lifted their long-flown scaffolds,

a bird-headed man floats, stick figure, as though he'd risen,
one beside one of his woolly extinctions—the vision, first
inkling glimmer—a primal sprout out of the monkey mind.

Above, new gods engrave their crooked crosses, yellow stars.
Let her sit awhile underground, alone, in silence with silence.
Let her lift her hand, once, to feel the Root-less at the root.

(The Nail)

Through the palm spread wide on the ruled beam jutting,
the point where the gouged plain floods between rivers,
the shaft descending, bloody, its head the ashen sky—

through the eye, lidless, a bright or bloodshot bauble,
the irises' flared corona, the pupil's feigned eclipse
into which the world plunges to swim inside the skull—

through the ear's occluded shell, the word wound inside
like a creature housed in its fear, its one claw reaching
to scuttle every light year vacant in its element—

through the tongue inside its cave, mute, un-mollified,
hung listless as a veil rent in the holy of holies,
or rag lifted, vinegar-soaked, toward the blistered lips—

through feet, folded, like hands in a downward prayer,
the planted trunk an axletree anchoring space to earth
that tilts over on its side like a reversal of the poles—

through the flesh, until what is left is a rank afflatus
rolling onward, outward from the tall stacks spewing,
and this night the toxic whiff of all things passing—

through, now, the mongrel armies swelling, swarming,
as on Arjuna's range by the one need, Force, as under
Troy's walls, Canaan's fields, Rome, this newest Reich—

and now through this woman who kindly craves the nail,
whose every breath's a plea to bring the hammer down,
the body done, forsaken, run through again, and through—

(Rue de Fleurus)
Gertrude Stein

"War is not so very near even when it is near these fields
where I have Alice reposition the cow my sentence's every
vantage a Cubist vector as one with whom some certainly

following I too am completely charming now in Belley the
children trooped to camps the earth covered all over with
people an awful lot of them I'm only interested in what

genius can say the rest anyway like killing five thousand
Anyones St. Theresa is not interested colored wine apple
plum carpet steak a piece a little piece please this is use and

identity is a funny thing funny you are never yourself you
do not believe yourself why should you since you know so
well so very well it is not yourself no obligation to recall

what is the answer what is the question no there is no there
there was that time not far from our Rue de Fleurus atelier
the paintings floor to ceiling Renaissance chair high backed

I saw her walking through the Jardin du Luxembourg like me
wearing pants like me loose workshirt Oh but waifish from
the Sorbonne perhaps or from the Rue Auguste Comte un-

likely to be positive positively like me a Jew so very unlikely
known communist to embrace Petain endorse Hitler like me
unlikely those days to come to my salon Picasso Apollinaire

Derain wives with Baby Wojums Mama Wojums enthroned
safe now in a prolonged present no need to leave France it
would be awfully uncomfortable and I'm fussy about food."

(Gravity)

To consider the storm trooper goose-stepping into Prague
not in the flicker chamber of a newsreel but in the flesh,
is he not the barnyard animal who by instinct, mechanical,

falls on the wounded hen? The hero in his gleaming armor
lives to anoint the enemy with his sword, while the saint
walks naked into the divagated center, that imploding star,

though how is it one can enter into surface, since all life
is lived in two dimensions, with its longing for the third
that appears, here, as the hollow one desires to fill—God

abandoned by God into gravity? And inside the vacuum
abhorred by nature, is that not the counter-lure of grace
for which one can only wait, willingly renouncing the will?

She leans in her room against the straight-back chair reciting
Love bade me welcome, the headaches surging in the place
where soul and body meet, a constant beating like the heart,

Yet my soul drew back, guilty of lust and sin, and what she begins
to feel, "a presence more personal, more certain, more real
than that of a human being," comes over her instantly—

Love's onslaught, unaccountable, and drawing nearer to her,
sweetly questioning, if she lacked anything, taking possession
"in the midst of my suffering," *a guest worthy to be here* and she

the guest, her hand taken, her self-taken *I cannot look on thee*
into the vacuum as, outside, Führers preen, soldiers parade
Come taste my meat, across their flatland, and she *did sit and eat*.

(Solesmes)

Eggshell, bone, swan's fleece pearl: lactescent statuary
in the Belle Chapelle, saints' bodies as though fast frozen
in stone, their eyes intent, hands gestural in their stillness,

arrayed there where the savior's being entombed, corpse
lowering on water, no, a winding sheet unfolded, flowing,
the mirror to his mother lowered at the transept's end.

April. Easter. Simone with *her* mother among the throng
come to hear the monks at prayer, their ancient chanting
the melisma aloft and blissful of time, eternity, each note

hurting her like a blow. So, she fixates, lets the splitting
ache inside her skull be what it is, flesh, heaps the flesh
where it belongs: into the corner. *Deus interior intimo meo,*

God closer to me than I am to myself, Beauty real, Truth real:
"In course of these services the thought of the Passion
entered my life, once and for all." And entering there, too,

as on stage, her two Englishmen, "angel boy," "devil boy,"
one handing her Herbert, radiance beaming from his face,
the other who dreamed he'd be a writer, handing her *Lear.*

What is the cross but a lever, "going down to rise up,"
while the whole universe weighs on us as on everything,
"and God the only counterweight" who comes over to us

"through the thickness of time and space"—coming now,
like light through stained glass where, for a thousand years,
walls have risen above this river, their likeness in its rush.

(A Pythagorean Notion)

Here, now: God the architect, God geometer. As on the icon
where the First Person, robed (the cross of the Second blazing
inside His halo) stoops with his compass over the portioned

cosmos that appears like an ovum at the bottom of the frame.
No, into it as though in vitro, ordinal, numerary, inseminating
the primordial with the golden symmetries, lucent, perpetual,

and gravity "the work of creation." Whereby God through love
"ceases to be everything" so that there might be something,
and God present in each as in a host, or by a code, Tetradic,

triangle inside a circle inside a square (the Third's presence)
at the core, and at the center the body outreaching, Vitruvian—
nothing ever in its own becoming not wholly a part of God.

Though from here everything looks wholly apart from God,
like the tortured naked body on its cross, forsaken, Vitruvian,
and matter itself an emptying through this broken symmetry,

the universe "a case of contradictions," both of them true,
God and No God: "for there is nothing that resembles
what is conceived when I say the word." And so every bridge

is a tearing asunder, the tree of knowledge a real tree, the tree
of life a wooden beam, track along which the centuries pass
like trains, already a mind, twisted, designing the ashen camps

and, at the fringe, Simone feels the hot iron singeing her brow.
Soon now, millions of randomly angled bags, piled, pyramidal,
wait timelessly for carriers at the last gate, traveling nowhere…

(Little Portion)

In the eye between the Anchluss and blood-fires of Guernica,
(like a brilliant point of light beyond the Duce's folded arms),
she has entered the *chiesetta*, Porziuncola, "the little portion"

where the saint would kneel in prayer, where the raw wounds
scored themselves into his feet and hands, his palms open,
arms stretched wide, like one who embraced the firing squad—

tracer rounds of love shot from God's body to his own.
Not in the great church, "abominable," built around this cell,
not under the high dome's atmosphere, but hunkered here

she feels for the first time, alone, "something stronger than I"
(though isn't God "withdrawn from the universe" powerless
within it?) that compels her now to go down on her knees.

Outside, Brother Sun pours over Umbrian hills his canticle
of light, Sister Moon hides patiently behind day's blue veil,
while Brother Wind and Sister Water flow down and through

the olive trees on the low descending slopes of Sister Earth.
Somewhere, under Brother Fire's stars, the saint is preaching
to his congregation of birds, and all the wolves of Gubbio,

benignly murderous, bowing, offer their paws to his hands.
And if it must be sacrificed, this nothing, this created self
like the saint in his *transito*, is it only cold matter sifting

into itself again, swap of energies, the nameless Zero Sum,
not the sudden combustion of bluebirds from a raven flock
as Little Sister Bodily Death calls all her playmates home?

(Firmament)

"God's Adamic touch, the Banishment, Michelangelo's skin—
the haunt of the world entire on this sky's exploded view,
magnificent, like the rapt soul's projection of a firmament.

I lay half on my back as André advised, breaking the rule,
and argued sharply with the guard! Dear family, if Paradise
is like St. Peter's, the Sistine choir, it is worth going there."

Three days she strays the capital, Palatine, Forum, Coliseum,
"dead drunk on Greek statues," San Anselmo's "pure jewel,"
Di Vinci's *St. Jerome* on wood—her rucksack tour of Rome

through palimpsests of empire, early, late, profane, sacred,
and that ardent Fascist student who had been told of her:
"very naïve, the poor fellow, I must have left him gasping....

I would prefer starvation in a salt mine to the slim horizon
of these young people, that cave less stifling than the brute
adoration of power, or some masked deification of death."

Though to remember Florence, the Uffizi: "overwhelming,"
the Botticellis, but nothing "to equal Giorgione's *Concerto*,"
its figure glancing heavenward, fingers ranging the keys—

beautiful people among beautiful things, beauty of the world,
is it grace, its superabundance? The mouth of the labyrinth
where, at the center, God waits to eat those who desire?

Go ask the lutenist's son, belated Galilean, one scope aimed
above, the other into depths—vastness bridging vastness
along the spectrum-thin medium of Earth. And still it moves.

(Rue des Grands-Augustins)
Pablo Picasso

"Between my first name and last, a litany of saints unfolds
like patrons in a deck of prayer cards—Maria of the Cures,
Cyprian of the Holy Trinity, Joseph, Francis, James, John,

mother, father—so many, I might be my own apostolate!
I am who I am—Minotaur pontifex of this apostate world
who ventures any tangent out to make the greatest art—

from the cave walls of Dordogne to Bosh to Goya to this,
my *Guernica*. See how the gored horse rears and screams,
how the dismembered soldier stretches, knife in one hand,

stigma in the other, how, arms raised, the screeching one
burns alive in gray fire as the grieving woman floats below
the bull's head, agonizingly, as though rapt in carnal ecstasy,

with the bull looking off into space as if into a mirror,
the ghost face, the torturer's light bulb, the All-Seeing
hovering over all. This bull is a bull, this horse a horse.

Don't ask the meaning, though if I wished I could paint
like Da Vinci, in his *Last Supper*, all tangents converging
on the Christ's face, serene, the hidden form Pythagorean.

In mine you can see, subliminal, that ghostly human skull:
*The infinite, which is in man, is at the mercy of a little piece of iron,
the whole being stricken, a harrowing pain, and no place for God.*

That is something of what I heard she said, she who I saw
crossing the Gardens, cistern eyes not unlike my Dora's.
I could paint her, riven ensemble, gazing beyond the frame."

(Rio Ebro)

After turning away from the rearguard of Paris, the safe
house of her pacifism, with her parents following, afraid
she will do something silly, after descending with the militia

through Lerida into Aragon to the banks of the Ebro
to take up her rifle there, her comrades at target practice
fleeing anywhere near her line of fire (*Lord deliver us*

from mousey women); after crossing to the other side
where Phalangists wait in this war without prisoners
"for if one is captured, one is dead," she hugs ground

only to look up—stretched out on her back as the spitfire
flies past on reconnaissance, thinking she will be caught—
and sees nothing other than the increase of blue sky,

this "infinity of perfect beauties, of all things that were
or will be" and looks for an instant "beyond the veil
to the real presence," objectless, adoring the distance

(though "all the horrors of this world are like the folds
imposed on waves by gravity") between God and God:
until the stooping man one thinks one sees on the road

at dusk reveals a tree, and the voices heard just leaves
rustling on *Los Picos Trés Marias* where the river begins—
before the bivouacs resume and she burns herself with oil,

before her comrades who will fight and die carry her out,
before her parents who did not expect to see her again
see her again, arrived safely, smiling, radiant: "Here I am."

(Screen)

This flicker-shimmer in the cave's wide dark: a figure lifts,
the little tramp born days before the Führer, dead ringer
in *The Great Dictator*. Though, now in *Modern Times*, Simone,

entranced, watches Chaplin, frenetic on the assembly line,
wrench tight the speeding widgets as they madly pass apace.
And now he's riding the conveyor, cog born to implement

the single feature of his job inside the great machine until
he's swallowed down this hungry one of many rote mouths
into the gear works, one of the yield, wheels within wheels

ingesting him then reversing, spewing him back out again
along the belt onto factory floor, so he sees everywhere
only bolts to tighten on bodies, faces—human material,

fleshly commodity. She leaves the theatre. Paris, summer.
Before Anschluss, Berchtesgaden. Before a crooked cross
hangs inside the keyhole parabola of the Arc de Triomphe:

"Only Chaplin understands the worker's plight in our time,
civilization broken, uprooted, with the spirituality of work,
good broken, scattered, hell itself nothing but false infinity."

The counter mechanism? The mustard seed, least of seeds,
rising upward by consuming itself, "irresistibly ascending,
attaining light"—analogy that makes this world, darkly,

in another Image: as the Great One swirls balloon globes
in his arms, and the overture wends ahead, and he dances,
dancer, dance, around the flat blank country of the screen…

A Native in this World

There is only one fault: incapacity to feed upon light, for where capacity to do this has been lost all faults are possible....

SIMONE WEIL

(Processions)

Nascent silence. Above the sea, a full moon ripples its light
into folds of waves, the same light falling like powdered silver
on the village where women, candles in their hands, voices

lifting the ancient hymns, move in procession to the shore
to bless the boats. *No céu desponta nova luz*—in the sky dawns
new light? Something sadder, Simone believes, heart-rending,

for the village is "wretched," and what is borne in upon her
confirms what she has known: the red-hot iron, the mark
of the slave, given to the afflicted, with the religion of slaves.

On her first day in her first factory in her year of factory work,
she had arrived in a white blouse; the workers saw her hands,
soft, as yet unscarred—a student who had failed her exams?

Not this professor with her "inborn awkwardness" offering
herself to the machines, like a copper bobbin to the furnace,
flames licking fingers, arms, her unable to close the shutter:

unable, at one shop then another to meet the need for speed,
to work without thought, like the cutter slicing her thumb,
the mill that drives the metal shaving in her palm—slavery

"not in the circumstances, but carried by the work itself"—
her upset at seeing the conveyor belt, its frantic procession
under the pendulum, the human cognates at their given task...

All most unlike this living circle of women walking, singing
around their husband's boats, again, now, for centuries,
a full moon, the sea below rippling light. This nascent silence.

(String)

Not the village, south of Viana do Castello, not the blessing,
but the whine of turbines in the factory's packed clatter-box—
Alstom, Langlois, Luchaire, Salmson, Gevelot, Renault…

So, she makes rounds to bring herself under: her "project"
to know the workers' true estate at bobbin-furnace, belt,
stamping press and mill, having cast her lot with all those

destined by duress, yet amazed to see the women gossiping
after work, "chattering" while she in "a cold fury" walks
to the Seine, wondering if she were "condemned to this life"

could she resist "throwing herself in?" And rouge applied
to her lips, rose to her cheeks, to coax managers to hire her:
one "with his carved head, twisted, tormented, monastic":

even whips succumb to affliction, the human humiliated.
Consider as postulate a metaphor: all creation an open string,
every note thrumming in relation on the scale, ratio, octave

by octave, playable because of the string. Love is the string,
vehicle and tenor, affliction the far strut "where violence
turns to suffering"—harm harmonized in privation of God.

But to have this condition plucked, plucked again and again,
what note will be raised? "The resigned docility of the beast
of burden: to be born to wait, receive, and carry out orders…

And always, one's need for the *external* signs of one's value."
Cue the truth of force, inescapable, the Revolution doomed.
Cue the Jacob's ladder of the freighter to Portugal and Spain.

(Papa Trotksy)
Bernard Weil

"Dear L, It perhaps will not surprise you that the Bellevilles
have dismissed Simone—she would not change her clothes,
would not wash her hands to milk the cows, would eat little,

would, beyond all tact, ask these humble people questions
no one should: *How do you manage? How much do you make?
What do you desire?* This latter most embarrassing to them.

Then the endless talk in the fields, of poverty, deportations,
the future martyrdom of the Jews, of the war she foresees
that will engulf the whole globe. So much for Bourges.

Though 'the best thing is to be nothing,' you understand
how she brooks no orthodoxy. Recall the German refugee
she had us lodge at Auguste Comte? We never can say no.

Just so, more emphatically, when Trotsky joined the house
that New Years, 'Papa' and his son 'The Crown Prince,'
'Papa,' his main flattened with pomade, his goatee shaved,

dressed like one of the bourgeoisie, he ventured out to see
the Eisenstein, and his bodyguards' revolvers propped
on our armchairs. In the next room when they returned,

we heard Papa's shouts, and Simone, coolly calm, stinging
her reproach. And she, a Trotskyite who wrote for *Le Verite*—
'A child,' Sedova exclaimed, 'holding her own with Trotsky!'

My child, twenty-four then, who in the old photograph sits
in my lap in Mayenne, my hands around her waist, her hand
on my knee, eyes fixed, her face half in shadow, half in light."

(Force)

NOTHING ENTERS HERE THAT IS NOT GEOMETRY,
block letters traced above the classroom door by her students
in Roanne, ordered for removal, though outside, under the cedar

that casts a shadow over them, they "discuss in perfect freedom."
Her reason for hope? "To understand the force that crushes us,"
the Reichstag burnt, a calculated ruin, the new Chancellor risen

out of the ash, hate, like a tuning fork, sharpening its pure note
to Krystallnacht, transports, wrath, onslaught. In time, she sees
the mechanism, how it works, brutal, how humans, even gods

can make themselves but things, the world a poem of force
with force the only story, the only actor, only hero: as when,
enraged, Achilles affords his vengeance to the surging river,

its currents wrung red with blood, banks slung with corpses,
hacked flesh nibbled by fish, a torrent seething downstream
till the river dams with bodies and they block its path to sea,

the river rearing up, wrathful, gushing to slay the god-man—
so force mounts without measure or equilibrium, its rush
and flood not heroic, not now: firebombs, lightning war,

factory work mastered to groove a pure symphony of death.
No, not now: Berlin before the coup, at the café where she sits
waiting for her parents. Is she thinking of how nature drowns

the inner life like Niobe, her children killed, and, still, she eats?
"Just a few uniformed Nazis on the streets, and they behave
like everyone else." A thought, passing, under the beech trees.

(Red Virgin)

High on her volcanic spur above the city, coral-colored bronze,
barefoot, she stands on the globe, crushing the snake beneath,
in her arms the child savior, on her head a crown of stars—

such-like is the postcard Simone posts to Bouglé at the École:
"We shall send the Red Virgin as far away as possible, leave her
to fashion bombs for the coming grand convulsion, and never

hear of her again." Delighted, she settles at Le Puy, teaching,
students noting her "natural inelegance," sweaters worn back-
wards, her clumsiness, a look "piercing" through thick glasses,

how she emanates "a total frankness and forgetfulness of self."
Days she teaches Plato, geometry, writes evenings for *L'Effort*:
"In Marx's eyes, the most important conquest of revolution

should be the abolition of work broken, degraded into kinds,
intellectual, manual." But to shake hands with stone-breakers,
to teach math to coal miners, congress with workers in cafes,

to presume to organize the unemployed? "The proletarians
don't need Joan of Arc. Let her do her job and keep her place."
"The Anti-Christ is at Le Puy—a woman dressed like a man."

"Meetings at the Labor Exchange preceded the demonstration,
led by Mlle. Weil, bearer of the Muscovite gospels, red virgin
of the tribe of Levi, brainwashing wretches she leads astray."

"The trolless stays up every night," her mother writes to father,
"and has the same absurd ideas on what maids should be paid.
Can you see her a mother? No, I don't think she's marriageable."

(Rue Auguste Comte)

From the terrace, clockwise: Eiffel Tower, Chaillot, the dome
of the Invalides, Arc de Triomphe, Sainte-Clotilde, the towers
of Saint-Sulpice, the Opéra, the Louvre; then counterclockwise,

leftward: Sainte-Chapelle, Saint Jacques, Pantheon, Sorbonne.
The Gardens like a vernal carpet unspool to the Palace below.
Twelve o-clock across the Seine: Monmartre and Sacré Coeur,

three calcite mitres above the cave where martyrs' bodies rest.
Simone, with a lantern, climbs stairs to her parents' apartment
bought from blueprints, as yet unfinished, on a street named

for someone positive the past is better passed over, passed away—
positive "the primitive mind" will evolve to richer knowledge
to material laws beyond godly fictions: his religion of humanity.

Now, at the École, she writes her *topoi*, probing: "What is work?"
"Action that is divided…implying an *extended* world that holds
the *desired* from us, distancing the future…shaping time, space."

Postulate, thus, her *cogito*: "I *can* therefore am," but *I* don't exist,
"only so far as I participate in the all-powerful.…" And God
"pre-supposed, posited by right action and in no other way"—

her Marxism thus haunted, gospel ghost in the material machine,
its roulette starts and eshatons. Do you see her descending
to where the barges unload their freestone below the Austerlitz,

see her among chiseled blocks, chain smoking, kneeling there
beside the floodwall, the few beggars paying no mind, hair
brushing her face, blots like paint spatters on a stained blouse?

(The Martian)
Simone de Beauvoir

"Simone et Simone—we met each other while we prepared
to enter the Normale: Athériou, a third Simone. No one,
I'm sure, would mistake we three for a simulacrum of one.

She, Weil, intrigued me: her great reputation for intelligence.
She would stroll around the Sorbonne courtyard, attended
by a group of Alain's former students, in one jacket pocket

a copy of *Libres Propos,* in the other a copy of *L'Humanité.*
She cried, I was told, when she heard of the Chinese famine.
Those tears compelled me more than her philosophy. To her

one thing mattered—the Revolution to feed all the starving
of the Earth. I remember how she looked me up and down,
snapping: 'It's easy to see that you have never gone hungry.'

And her bizarre outfit! Clearly, she was determined to live
as much as possible like a man, as if it were her misfortune
to have been born a female. No wonder, so I've been told,

that Alain who, surely, she revered, called her 'le Martien,'
the kind one finds in H.G. Wells: just all eyes and brains.
Still, a woman is not born but made, as I myself have said.

Surely, she was no incidental being, Simone, whom I envy
for having a heart large enough to beat around the world.
'What I cannot understand is how one can't believe in God,'

so, I'm told she said. I don't believe in God, inclined as I am
to father's paganism over my mother's faith—*this* Simone,
heart beating for more lovers of both sexes than I will name."

(Fable)

Wind flower, anemone, summoned by the goddess's tears:
when the lost king stumbles on a forest hut, he finds her,
the beautiful sister of six brothers changed by a stepmother

into swans; he falls in love, and both make their way back
to his kingdom where he weds her, and she bears a child,
a child the stepmother also steals. To prove her innocence,

she must spin six shirts from the frail white petals to restore
her brothers to human form, to restore her child, and, so,
for six years, she must not speak, cannot acquit her silence.

Just as she will be put to death, swans appear, she throws
the six shirts over them, and they assume human shapes,
all revealed, evil exposed, the kingdom, the family, saved.

Such, the young daughter in the lycée writes, is the only way
to gain power—by keeping silent to weave the impossible—
a singular concentration. For purity, so already she believes,

is the world's only strength: its diamond, its true worth
more precious than admixtures or iridescent silks. *And God,
my precocious Simone, who is God?* Not God-object, the God

that exists, but the God that must be. *And is it to this God
you pledge your faith?* To the God I seek who never seeks me.
How should one live? Like Alexander who, brought a cask

of water, poured all onto sand to share his soldiers' thirst.
So, all takes place inside the soul, the free act. *Is God freedom?*
Yes. And I am as alone with this God as I am without him.

(Tooth)
André Weil

"A brother is like a tooth, Simone would say, a good thing,
provided one is not too often forced to know that it exists.
Though in those early photographs we seem inseparable—

like the one in Penthièvre after the War, I must be twelve.
She, just nine. That picket fence behind like a trench marker.
It is hard to say which of us looks more awkward, her head

tilted in that bob-cut she kept ever after, me with my book,
arms stiff at my sides, both in shorts. Or the one at Mayenne
where father was stationed, on the sunlit path, our shadows

stretching out in front of us like our futures, the sun's angle
higher behind her, so her shadow runs longer up to the edge.
She's leaning on me, away from me in the first. In the third,

she is two, I am five. She is wearing a dress, I, a sailor's suit.
We hold hands, the way we'd knock on villas in Jullonville
pretending to starve: 'Our parents will let us die of hunger!'

'Poor children' the people said and gave us candy and cake.
Was it in Mayenne, that it began, our divagation? No, later—
mother's friend who nodded to me: 'One is genius itself,'

then to Simone: 'the other beauty.' Migraines started after.
I taught her Greek for the fable she wrote, *The Fire Imps*—
her first—flames transfiguring to dancers dying away, then

flaring into life again. Our trolless, I'd dub her later, our imp,
my sister who'd tell us, last we saw her: 'Had I several lives,
I'd have devoted one of them to you, but I have only one life.'"

(Garden)

"These designs attributed to God are cuttings made by us,
chosen from infinite turns, connections that might be made
by any intelligence, human, non-human, no matter the scale,

throughout space and time…" Let this cutting be morning
in the Luxembourg Gardens: They have come by streetcar
across the Seine—son, mother, baby Simone who refuses

to be fed, except by bottle, holes cut in the nipple to let
solid foods pass. Not yet two. Sickly. *This baby cannot survive.*
Each day they walk the paths so she breathes the fresher air,

this intricate parterre of flowers and lawn, the central basin
with its water jet, these balustrades, the marionette theatre—
like an unbroken symmetry… And people sitting, passing,

as in a painting by Watteau. Is she looking at the toy boats?
At the play of light in the pool? Among terraces and statuary,
fountains plash, wind flicks the trees, and four bronze bodies

hold the world on its axis… Here is the path she will name
for Rousseau, wild, where she will love to walk with friends.
But where is that other, where the stranger reveals himself,

is she on her way to lycée? "An incident without importance,"
André will say; "That business," she'll say, "that birthed in me
revulsion, humiliation at being desired." And *this* cutting,

this insult to the one life? Does it fix the purity of a glacier?
The extravagance of the mustard seed, a longing to eat light?
Round, round goes the carousel. Bees in the beehouse hum.

(Rue du Paradis)

"I am giving birth to something" she'll declare, though now
she is midway on from that single sphere Plato had devised—
here, in Grandmother Weil's apartment on Rue du Paradis

where the family gathers, called by her who still keeps faith—
prayers they will chant at sunset to One Who Is Everywhere.
Her son, the doctor, has brought wife and son, called *L'enfant*

as though he were the world's one child, has brought them
with tact, not wanting to chide his mother's piety: *Praise You,*
Your command brings dark to evening…You order the cycles of time…

You order the stars on their rounds…You create day, You create night,
Rolling away light before darkness…Praise You for the evening dusk.
A piano begins—Mime Weil? Her mother?—its risen notes.

"When we listen to Bach the soul's powers turn tense, silent,
to apprehend this thing of perfect beauty…." But the one
who speaks has barely begun beginning, like all, in scales:

blood rivering its circuits to light the womb's cave—one
from two, single cell, two from one, three, four, so one
ascends descending, bridge to bridge, until there is Simone:

What do you want in life? The teacher will ask her. *Do not forget*
plants grow out, not only up. And she years later nearing death:
"Fruits, leaves are wastes of life if one wants to go higher."

For to leave the cave is to be cut off, is to fasten on hunger.
For there is silence in the universe like noise compared to God's.
For even now the keys go quiet, quiet, like a sun standing still.

...and Silence after, the exceeding music
into which all hunger passes like a ripple

of the one current in shore-less ocean,
its waters neither surface nor undertow

in which the worlds swim ceaselessly,
and nothing moving there unminded...

THREE

At the Grave of Teilhard de Chardin

Most painful is the absolute silence of all our scientific investigations towards our questions concerning the meaning and scope of the whole display. The more attentively we watch it, the more aimless and foolish it appears to be. The show that is going on obviously acquires a meaning only with regard to the mind that contemplates it. But what science tells us about this relationship is patently absurd: as if mind had only been produced by the very display that it is now watching and would pass away with it when the sun finally cools down and the earth has been turned into a desert of ice and snow.

ERWIN SCHRÖDINGER

But what an absurd thing life is, looked at superficially, so absurd you feel yourself forced back on a stubborn, desperate, faith in the reality of the survival of the spirit. Otherwise—were there no such thing as the spirit, I mean—we should have to be idiots not to call off the whole human effort.

TEILHARD DE CHARDIN

Born in Auvergne, France, in view of an ancient landscape of extinct volcanoes, Teilhard de Chardin was a geologist, paleontologist, and priest whose work was instrumental for the exploration and science of early human origins during the first half of the twentieth century. While studying theology at Ore Place in Hastings, England, in 1911, he read Henri Bergson's *Creative Evolution*, which had a profound effect on his thinking. The book was banned by the Church the following year. His experience as a stretcher bearer during the First World War also had a profound impact on his ideas about humanity in a laborious and painful process of spiritual evolution. Though his scientific work rose to great prominence, his extensive religious and spiritual writings met with resistance and censure by the Vatican—in particular his groundbreaking embrace of evolution as an indubitable theory of life consonant and supportive of his theological vision. Unpublished during his lifetime, though circulated among friends and admirers, his collected theological, devotional, and speculative works became pervasively influential after his death on Easter Sunday 1955 after a life of almost ceaseless journeying.

As in a Vivid Sleep

No, you do not ask anything unattainable of me. You merely, through your revelation and your grace, force what is most human in me to become conscious of itself at last. Humanity was sleeping—it is still sleeping—imprisoned in the narrow joys of its little closed loves.

TEILHARD DE CHARDIN

Let the inhabitants of the rock sing...

ISAIAH, 42:1

(His Stone)

Again, this dawn-lit incandescence through the yew trees,
and down the slope, the river scrolling the length of itself
in every purl and ripple. When, years ago, they set me

to attest his life among the growing human increase
under grass, I had long been lifted from the groundmass,
soft-grained, sun-blanched, vaguely crystalline, his name

cut into me plainly with his beginning and his end,
and the frozen earth unwilling to lay him to his rest
for this man to sleep the sleep of trust, the sleep of seed

in the winter field. "It is a terrifying thing to be born,
to find oneself, without having willed it, swept along,"
still, I hear him say, "on a torrent of fearful energy."

Or maybe I only think I hear him, as if I were his god
of iron, a childhood's distant dream, infinitely durable,
not my weathering granite shield against effacement.

What comes at the very end, he said, is the adorable.
To this pad-locked field behind the shuttered church
I watch them swing the gate and scan the identical rows

along the tarred path pillowed by decades of moss
until they find me, each one leaving their gift of stone
on my crest. And sometimes it is, in that stillness,

as if I am the river moving along with the layers,
light pouring over me, pouring through me, light
speeding from so far away it has no past or future.

(Puy-de-Dôme)

The late foragers wouldn't know what to make of me
erupting as I did from deepest earth, building myself,
plumes and fire out of ash, my rush of living magma

leveling virgin forest for new growth when I cooled.
No wonder, after they finally left the caves, rooved
their sheds, gathered the herds, when conquerors

cleared roads, they raised a temple at my cinder crown
to the god of boundaries, god of messages and trade,
a blended god, the soul's guide to the underworld.

Am I not the emblem of all that was or will be, all
embers born of embers from a primal blinding flash,
and harbinger for the tallow sun flickering out?

He must have known as much, must have intuited,
that boy who would climb my bluff hoping to find
"what there was inside the volcanoes," pouring over

my share of earth, its rocky sediments, crystal-veins,
as though he would harvest every stone, shell-splinter,
metal bolt, the lock-pin of a plough—his succession

"of idols" before his iron god. *Fiery their force, celestial
their home*, reads the family's adage, with that trinity
of roses above the lintel their seal, such pretentions

of their kind. Yes, he would see through me, the boy
who would call himself a pilgrim along a road of fire—
see into my obdurate heart to the flaming heart beyond.

(Wake)

If, as Plato dreamed, time is just a moving image
of eternity, am I not then the glittering trailing ripple
of a world-line through matter passing on ahead?

Or imagine, if you will, my life on this coarser scale,
the character of a quantum riptide behind the stern,
bubbling into being through this fluid interference

of currents that become a Gulf, this Sea called Red
where the scientist, this priest, follows on his exodus
between Sinai and the Nile, an array of fossil bones

where the holy family made their timorous flight
into the desert, its shifting rush of saffron, a startle
of snipes from the tamarinds, spray of mimosa—

then, as now, a sudden heron skimming the shore's
milky wash, nets of fishermen seizing the moment
as I would fold everything gathered into my present.

Not far below, hawksbills cruise the underwaves,
chordata roam the glass-strung cathedrals of reefs
that are venerable as sacred cities, mineral, animal,

living and dead, releasing a blizzard of softest flesh
to dwarf the work of Giza above, these architects
more ancient than any pedaled upstart—but blindly?

Matter, spirit: two aspects of the one stuff, this priest
supposed—and mind in harness all the way down.
Still: gunshots like pocked Braille on the Sphinx's face.

(The Weald)

And if a *shaw* could speak, what would it say, my name
eponymous for what is left of the lost great forest
born out of rock a hundred million years ago, sandstone,

clay veils and outcrops from the scoured Cretaceous dome,
given by the late arrivals, *weald, wold*, my first dwellers
driven west—words tapped from the tongue's one root?

Though not first: what of the saurians, iguanodons, teeth,
bones, shells sifted from fells, escarpments? An eye's blink
to me. From Ashdown sand beds and Gault formations

came the pannages and droveways, transhumaning lines
inclining to forge and waterwheel, that scrupulous genius
inveigling the strata to materialize his species' *Origin*.

Scrupulous, too, this other who saw in the same strayed
mansions of matter the impossibility of anything alone—
who came to see in the rise of every form what's hidden

revealed through all the fragile congruencies of chance,
creation unfinished, incarnation unceasing, and grace
rising "like sap from one trunk into many branches."

How he watched with greatest patience that wood owl
outside Ore Place, watched a trinity of storks in flight,
or pored through quarries with his microscopic eye,

seeing in a moment the world in evolution, the whole
current of the cosmos in which he moved, moving
with earth and light on his sunset walks in the Weald.

(A Moon on the Front)

At night, when I wake, I am a blind man's Cyclopic eye
safe in my sky-perch above the barbed wire, the trenches,
rising here beyond this swarming maelstrom, this maul,

the species' bloody caul, the slough of its scored becoming:
I who tore myself free of the Earth, its molten offspring
tempered to shining dust and the poets' petulant dreams.

This one, this scientist, this priest, asleep in his shell-hole,
carries with him through the Hell below a double of me,
the lifeless host he knows to be the spirit's flesh and furnace.

Brancardier, stretcher-bearer, some call him Sidi Marabout,
straight-backed as a stele, with the face of an El Greco,
shielded, the sharpshooters say, by the *baraka* as he climbs

over ridge and parapet lifting the broken, the butchered,
non-believer, believer—if he dies he will "just be changed"—
all a part of the human magnitude, "the psychic current

of the universe" for "Eternal-Being-itself is everywhere
in process of formation *for us*." Ypres, Dunkirk, Verdun:
if he's killed, he said, mold his body to the redoubts' clay

like "mortar laid by God for the stones of the New City."
Soon, along the splayed and cratered tree line the unforged
light assumes again its precedence, while he imagines I am

a figure for the planet's slow awareness growing, passed
hand to hand, mind *en marche*, and the world the battlefield,
with seasons, rivers, meadows, the perfume of dead leaves.

(Shell)

Spira mirabilis, miraculous spiral, and from the one
infinite point my many chambers flowering inwardly
to form the outside this itinerant holds in his hand.

What am I but a translation of symmetries awakened
from the violin wavelengths of things coming to be,
not condemned to drift among possible impossibilities

like so many dead ends in shale, some Bright Angel
or Burgess, a petrified chamber on the planet's scale,
four hundred million years a wink to my pinhole eye?

When he looks in my lustrous emptiness does he see
how close he is with his kind never to have been at all,
chance roll from the compass-angle palm of the divine?

Still, I am the ensemble that redoubles sum by sum
into pinecone-bract and sunflower—golden array
of assemblages, each uncurling like a fern, unlikely

in their aspects till the eye shoots deeper in—even
their outspread numbered branching on the Earth
a kinship with the kinship of more hidden symmetries.

What will he hear when he lifts me to that near twin
and his inquisitive crown leans closer and he presses
me against the hollow in himself—an ancient wish?

Or this ocean-rush of pre-dawn nothings whispering,
hushing out? Or will it be the true God in all that is,
living and incarnate, altogether apart, not far away?

(Lattice)

His wrestling with me is inside, though the errant
wastes beyond the Great Wall assume the vivid cast
of soul, trawling emptiness, terrain in which he sifts

his beginnings from brickearth and loess, sheer-flung
ramparts of Aeolian dust where the species quartered
long ago, not so long in its primordial glimmerings.

Knuckle-bone, skull-shard, the patiently-honed edge
of a blade, sheer-gleaned, wholly lithic, he carries back
across the Yellow River to the museum at Tientsin—

all belated relics of the beast who knows he knows,
while the remnant of me slips fleetly from the sieve,
quartz-chaff, first replicator, to run away on the wind.

Still, my older brethren celebrate a silence of lattices
cooling out of liquid into emerald and amethyst,
diamond facets in which the slightest flaw catalyzes

to greater beauty, azure mist from pure translucence
ghosting the stone. Am I not these lowlier tessellations
folding inside the very fabric of things, wanton tilings

crossing even from the inanimate into life, a feigning
of firm ends? Here is the helix with its rooted tapestry
of ties, far-flung from the materials, routed, branching,

the soul inseparable from the universe of being born,
infinitesimal, with the labors of seaweed, the industry
of bees at their hive-work, sweet honey from the rock.

(Current)

In this river's perpetual haste, I am already always
arrived, always already departed, the constant
wanderer among the hosts of different worlds,

arrow and mark, the course through which I make
things to make themselves, everything irreversible,
the syntax in the enzyme's shape, the atom's charges

composing from within into a grammar of things—
autocatalysis of particle into molecule into cell
until the eyes form the way swirls form in water,

patterns risen out of patterns, until the patterns
desire to know. This sweeping out of savannahs,
over continents, across steppes—their driven waves—

attests the spur: my own long indigent venture on.
Take this one with his kit-box, his tools, the pressed
moons of bread he keeps to offer Mass, he's shuttled

from Auvergne to Egypt, Sussex to Belgacom,
has barged the Huang-ho, mule-trained the Gobi,
yet he knows all of space "is a veil without a seam."

Though now he looks from his museum window
at the cedars along the Jardin des Plantes—again
Paris, in autumn, his favorite season, his specimens

on shelves in the room next door, books, oak desk,
a prospect of widening scope, of mind, planetary,
sky-bent like that antelope horn, pearled, spiraling.

(Garment and Corpus)

Most of what I wear no one can see, my nakedness
the nothing ghosting each barely probable array
from lack to leap to face to galaxy, till all you know

collapses into now: what this man called the bloom
of matter's marvelous garment in the flesh, a brede
just visible on the edge of what will be, was and is.

To walk these bustling human streets, to go astray
in Shanghai, Louvain, Paris, and Rome, or clamber
breccia, to find in the teeming dishabille and shards

some sidelong glancing image of my resplendence,
one must have a sightline honed by longing love
that would stitch in its bright gaze what came before

and what will come ahead, and so fathom the circuit
from the arrow of the line—my haunt, my harrowing:
like particles of light fired through a regnant screen,

each double of the other launched to opposite zones,
till the action of his science and the action of his faith
keep impossible counsel across the shattering gulf.

What vision, but mine, narrows the brash infinities
out of the improbable rattle bag of what might be,
warp, woof of a great Thought, not a great Machine?

He saw it first at the front in that dying soldier's eyes,
the agony like a plumb line down a bottomless well
ascending there with my own, transfiguring into joy.

(Fault)

I am the scandal inside the rock, the mist in bronze,
that makes the sculptor turn his hand, amend his eye
to find in stone's intended flesh the fortunate flaw.

I am the droplet mote of fog that sways and knocks
the pomegranate's alchemies about, diffusing them
to randomness, out of which anneals the very fruit.

I am the fabric's warp and woof, double life of loss
and growth, loss again, the passing names by which
each furthered world feels its life and knows its death.

I am the thread that webs itself through every maze
till I become the maze itself, and the walker there,
who mindfully, blindly, solely gropes the iron veil.

I am the stuttered origin, a gene-inflected molecule
conjuring futures from the acid soup, purposeless,
until this driven fraught machine divines the word.

I am the soldier's fall in each attack, the fatal block
that hides the manifold, inevitable, original, here,
endless, till No Man's suffers into Promised Land.

So, for eschatology, let this man descend the cave,
the cavern of beginnings below his own Dordogne,
to run his mind along that frieze of first imaginers,

the prey, the prime extinctions on the boss's fold
and fault—He thinks: *By means of all created things
the divine assails us, molds us.* With that assault, I am.

(Celestial Mountains)

Inside the great mirroring eye of my Heavenly Lake
I regard the wide ocean of my sky reaching out
along the glacial massifs and crystal heights of me,

God Mountain, Lord of the Spirits, Victory Peak
unraveled from the riven folds of Paleolithic faults
to ascend in watercourses, snowmelt tongues of ice,

network webs of streams and moraines that decline
to steppes, forests, redstarts and ringtails in the drafts
where underneath from their own pivoting sights

spread valleys of apricot and bitter apple, roe-deer
in migration where an instant ago, the foragers
came, dissimulating to Silk Road and trade route

east to west, west to east, sun-up and sun-down,
along the slow-shifting continent's ethereal spine.
This modern band encamped by the desert's edge

near the lamasery, the only road ahead blocked
with corpses and animals, talk together of God
whom the priest calls a choice between Yes and No

that no one can turn from—as the war rages on,
and far from my ridge the sandstorms bear down
to blind their caravan, ditched against the banks.

Out of entropy comes uplift: at the utmost height
my crystal pyramid reddening in sunlight; below,
his big hand opens like a flower to free the wheels.

At the End of Distances

I cannot look at the universe as a result of blind chance. Yet I can see no evidence of beneficent design, or indeed any design of any kind, in the detail. As for each variation that has ever occurred having been preordained for a special end, I can no more believe in it than that the spot on which each drop of rain falls has been specially ordained.

CHARLES DARWIN

(Hands)
George Barbour

"To fall forward stage by stage till the end of the world,
that's what he would say, my old friend with his kit-box
and breviary, his pack of Jobs, him chain-smoking them

year in year out from Tientsin to Transvaal, field notes
and skulls, his eyes keen for every jigsaw bit of bone,
Sinanthropus, Australopithecus, Miocene, Pleistocene,

all the way to this later infancy, this thinking envelope
of consciousness expanding, he held, like a living net—
one mind woven with all minds, drawn to the Ahead.

At Choukoutien I'd use crayons to track sediment
with colors on my notepad; he would keep gradations
like prisms in his head—drawings sharp as photographs.

Nights, at the fire, we would talk of his God of Tension
that carries the species on through every random spur.
Like that time on the steps of the Yamen, when a mule

struck him with its hind leg on the temple—the blister
the size of a bloody pigeon's egg—he quoted Li Po:
'It's as hard to travel in Szechuan as to climb to Heaven.'

And when my son died, near his own death, he wrote:
'I am convinced what looks like meaningless catastrophe
transforms itself into blessing.' And even those graves

at Tsinling, no stones, no names? Look at the hands,
spit-painted on cave walls, as if raised to brace a fall: No.
They're moving, they're making their way through rock."

(Fan and Spearhead)
Marguerite Teilhard de Chambon

"Like conifers in the Bois de Boulogne where he would walk
dreaming of Auvergne, home, the massif of Puy-de-Dôme
long before his exile east, that's how he envisioned the rise,

this progressive genesis of the universe, and of the human
phenomenon, across the fraught, material frontier into life,
and life, fanning, groping—directed chance—into thought.

When he would visit Clermont-Ferrand, my dearest cousin,
as a child, he would carry frogs for study into his bedroom.
Years later, I invited him to Rue de Fleurus, to my Institute

to school my girls on evolution, never mind what he called
'the cage of dogma,' mindful instead of truth's 'axis,'
and him knowing as I do—despite my male *nom de plume*—

the need to feminize the species. From the front, then,
he wrote to me of blasted ridges, of poplar trees misted
with gas, of this world recasting itself anew through battle.

For humankind is the spearhead, our restlessness not sin,
not the madness of a Faust, but the wake of some radial
energy drawing us forward out of un-life, and even there

mind is evident in the mesh of things before that deep
organic likeness stamps every creature. And then the like
of us steps fitfully down from the trees out of the grasses

wavering in sun and wind, out of our many twilit cousins
diverging, roving, dying out, as though God had scored
on the one tablet the same word for arrow and for life."

(We Thinking Reeds)
Auguste Valensin

"*In its depths I saw gathered, bound by love, the scattered leaves
of the universe*—Yes, how my friend loved his Dante,
seeing the very origin of the creative act as a channel,

a gate, the necessary entry, and this contingent matter
the chrysalis, though holy still: the living immanence
knotted within the within of things, the soul at once

the point of transformation and the arrow that makes
its way. For human being is not center but last born,
the leading shoot, we thinking reeds who have crossed

the threshold of reflection, this knowing that we know
and so—his faith and mine—a prospect scandalous
to entropy, unscathed by the system that runs with it.

Though at Aix with Blondel, or in Paris with Le Roy,
or at Villers-sur-Mer where he found that ammonite
crusted with clay, one could not ignore the extinctions.

Have they not now discovered spiked clay in limestone
where St. Francis tamed Gubbio's wolf with a word,
a fallen star's cataclysm—asterisk above the manger—

only one of many turns where the universe commits
abortion upon itself? And could we not be the next,
having swept the planet clean of many lives, spurred

by our restlessness to outstrip the rest, while the lost
recede in the wake of our wake, born to rush us ahead
like imperiled amphibians alive also in their double lives?"

(Ensemble)
Émile Licent

"The language of wings even in the hold of my nets
eluded me, was the limit for this listener: swallowtails
in brush lands when we'd leave behind the concession

to venture beyond the Great Wall into the Ordos.
And 'Teh,' as the locals called him, always thinking,
working borderlands between spheres of knowledge,

his science, his mysticism. Strange, to watch him eying
the escarpments, where Pei found the treasured skull
in travertine, so proficient in the past, still so pitched

to the future, what he saw to be the end of distances
where across infinities of scale the whole ensemble,
risen out of the random, from instinct into thought,

converges to its final cause. As for me, I collected
and prayed, expert in the language of what's required,
and built the needed thing in the time it was needed:

my museum, born out of the practicum of expedition,
not the wisps of vision. No wonder we sometimes
nearly came to blows. Still, technically, were one blest

to see down the bottom gneiss of things, see through
the layers like elemental parts of a language—words,
syllables, letters—to glimpse at once a substantial form

that had wrested mountains from the near nothing
below their base, sentience from loaded chemical dice,
persons from bacterium, would one not kneel in praise?"

(Fig)
Cardinal Merry del Val

"'I resign myself to the activity of a microbe,' he said
with the exile, the silencing, one twenty-year stretch
in China tending his rocks, caches of bones and tools,

divagating across a lifetime of more tools, more bones,
the work a well-intended speculation, barely samizdat:
'I shall swallow the obstacle in the act of my obedience.'

One must credit his faith, but our Holy Father saw best:
'I know Teilhard is a great scientist, but no theologian
to resolve the problem of God. There is no problem.'

The crux? He presumes God a contingent cause, limited,
thus, by His own creation, evolving with it as it were,
and sin, from the first, little more than necessary flaw,

more animal than original—a belated Pellegian goad—
that heals some time ahead with our long emergence,
and St. Paul's Christ like a cosmic strange attractor

that draws unto itself, already holy, the whole universe.
Consider for sin and heresy, then, the milieu of a fig,
the Garden's fatal fruit he believed an exemplary tale,

a figure for our fallible nature, transfigured over time—
Alpha lured by matter's turns to hierophant Omega.
Inside the fig is an inner realm of hothouse blossoms,

the fig's own world and telos, into which the fig wasp
crawls to lay its eggs, only enough so both might live,
lest the tree reject them. But the fig, the fig is not a fruit."

(Mirror)
Marguerite-Marie "Guigite" de Chardin

"When I read the draft of his *Milieu*, I knew the mirror
of my life in his had found new life in it: that sickness
never comes to diminish, but quickens God's own life

in us, us in God's life. As he reflects, 'Death's the sum
of all our diminishments, though we overcome death
by finding God in it.' And so it was for Alberic, Louise,

for Francoise, Gabriel, for us all, and my own affliction
a kind of brute spectacle that begets the inner flowering
that was my life at Sarcenat, as the Sacred Heart blazed

in the foyer, as it did when we were children, my body
bedridden thirty years, my life his dreamt *Imitatio Cristi*
while my dear brother crossed, crisscrossed continents

unerringly errant, arrow to my base on a compass rose.
As in de Hooch's imagined Delft, two figures travel
in mirror passages, one away from, one into the light,

or like mirror particles, chiral, contrarily handed, light,
again, invariant until its symmetry shatters ahead, so it is
in this looking glass world of scattered entanglements.

When I died, it was as though he was looking at Earth
from an immense distance, blue atmosphere, the green
of vegetation, then ever-more luminous—thought itself,

then ever deeper: the darkness of suffering, growing
sharper with consciousness, the widening inflorescence.
And God gazing out, gazing in at the flung reflections."

(Glass)
Bruno de Solages

"Our Lord said it truly: 'It is necessary scandals come.'
Though when I saw their crooked crosses *en marche*,
spreading virally through La Ville Rose, who could fault

the doubter in our midst demanding must *this* be so?
Everything that happens, I must own, is not adorable.
But to act like soldiers who fall in a battle that ends

in peace, that *can* be. For evil is inevitable in creation
that evolves in time. Such was what my friend believed
who taught that good can be salvaged from the worst.

It is true that when a wine glass falls from a table's end
it smashes into glints and shards, maybe the cracked
stem lists like a toppled column, and there is no way

to mend it back into the whole it was. Though it's true
as well—given the turns, the Janus-faced symmetries—
that the loss could reassemble like a movie in reverse,

the heat of its fracture, even a night of broken glass,
become the engine of its restoration. But the arrow
will not relent: I go as Jesus would have to the camp.

Now think of light through glass, its infinite prism,
is it not the same light streaming timelessly, forever,
through the whole intact as with every jagged part?

Reflective life ratchets on to what calls us on ahead:
the refashioning of our brokenness, though we live
incapable to see—Something—with us with Our Lord."

(Labyrinth)
Gabriel Marcel

"What did my rival call them, this host of living forms?
A labyrinth, incoherent, a maze of births and deaths,
ontogeny, phylogeny, until one perceives the thread,

the thread he called love, at the heart of the universe,
not sentiment but activity, with its groping into mind.
And with human mind the creation climbing on ahead.

'Provided a summit exists, and it is worth the climb,
what mountaineer,' he believed, 'wouldn't risk a fall?'
'Humans to be humans must try everything to the end.'

I balked at his Nietzschean metaphors, his Promethean
Christ, his 'eclipses of God,' and brooked the doctors
of Dachau as countermand to his flimsier figurations—

as if spirit could be wrung from a rabid consciousness.
Yet I too believed in humanity on the way, unbound
to wishful nets of furtherance, and founded on hope

of the present moment like a sudden clearing opening
in communion with another. Take for my labyrinth
this very Now as the floor before you, eleven circuits

woven into quadrants, and step into its foliate cross
as if it were the outward print of your own itineracy,
and let the center draw you to itself, its six rosettes

the soul of your awakening—approached, departed:
spiral bonds of snail shells, galaxies, blood and brain,
a cast of the Great Rose window and our harrowing."

(Thread)
Paul Valéry

"Where sails like doves flocked the ocean's glittering roof,
that's where I saw them swimming like refugees to shore
from the great foundering liner of their Church, the faith

battened against the death of God—I mean those faithful
who, too, took as irrefutable the depthless terminus of
this modern horizon. The abyss of history is big enough

for us all, I am unafraid to say, for I regard myself one,
as it were, founded on doubt. But the delightful Teilhard?
From the first, with Boule at the museum, then our talks,

I had to admire his spirit of adventure—to invent a faith
inside his faith, Christ as a sort of Cosmic Self, the God
of infinity toward which one must tend, where the thread

of the inward meets the thread of the outward, so always
we find ourselves at the exact point where all the forces
of the universe meet to weave the outcomes God desires.

I, contra, am post-hominin, and hold conscious existence
a zero from which we must diverge, and so cast my lot
with an invariant God, Einstein's, even if that God is dead.

In the end, the resurrection is the only dogma, our bodies
death-hollowed, emptied, to be remodeled in the fullness,
even if I don't believe it. Always it comes down, in the end,

to my graveyard by the sea, as to the valley of dry bones,
a skull-grinning gest in a molecular game, or something
like light through a high windowless sky lovingly endless."

(Icon)
Lucile Swan

"My precious: I loved the way he filled my name with light.
In liners churning endless west from east, east from west;
or in the Pir Panjal, or Mandalay, Bombay, some loop

of the Yangtze, his boat banking through an airy gorge,
he penned in letters that almost-other life I so desired,
but for his 'Something Else' that made us *trois* not *deux*.

Not that I wasn't deeply happy, not least the afternoons
we spent in my garden, rickshaws beyond the wisteria,
the Forbidden City near, our talks venturing everything

but our bodies—the pure contradiction of withholding
himself from me, we both agreeing that all matter lives,
the species evolves, only out of passion for the world,

a rhythm of time, the rhythm of the birth of the world:
PT, my pet-name, the man I'd dreamt to find all my life,
except God's joke of making him a priest. Like an icon,

in my portrait bronze of him I see the face of one gazing
beyond the verge, so what he sees in full convergence
is the species with the universe held in a living flame—

like the holy card he gave me when we parted, a heart
encircled by a crown of thorns, the lucent gold he saw
behind all things now vivid wholly at the parted center:

For 'by the love of man and woman a thread is wound
to the heart of the world,' and 'to grow towards the Light
each in the other, this is the future through space and time.'"

(La Cotte)
An Islander

"Not the grotto at Puerto Viesco, its red ochre paintings
of horses and deer, nor the rearing bison at Altimira,
their contours in chiaroscuro on Magdalenian stone:

Not the limestone honeycomb of hills near les Espas,
its "nuptial hall" where the man with reindeer antlers
and horse's tail strides by leopards in a lithe cortege,

nor Dragon Bone Hill, white quartz amidst the karst,
the slung-back skull of 'Nelly' beside ash and bones,
nor Sind, Irawaddy, Makapan—its Cave of Hearths:

But here, in the Channel, at La Cotte de Saint Brélade,
its collapsed granite headland of metamorphic rock,
did he glimpse the prospect of a past before the past.

That night, when we went fishing, under a risen moon,
I pointed out the passage, its jagged compass angle
gaping above the shingle. Inside, our latest cousins

mastered flint and fire, heavy-browed, bigger-brained
than us. Think of gazing out from those ranging eyes
for generations, their burial ground now under ocean

that then was rushing stream. 'Blessed are you, harsh
matter, stubborn rock,' he wrote that here, and held
the past is beautiful, but the future is more beautiful

than all the pasts. Then what is God, I would ask him?
And I see him now in caravan, turning: God, he says,
is a note of music, his hand tracing a spiral in the air...."

Like Glitter Ascended into Fire

In each one of us, through matter, the whole history of the world is in part reflected. And however autonomous our soul, it is indebted to an inheritance worked upon from all sides—before it ever came into being—by the totality of the energies of the earth...

TEILHARD DE CHARDIN

Thus, the whole universe appears as an infinitely small, and at the same time an infinitely large network of life forces which emanate from God and end in God, who is the source...

LÉOPOLD SENGHOR

Ψ

Bless me, father. What is this old, shattering emptiness
as if a cavern had opened inside, so with everything
I find myself infinitesimal, harrowed into "a past abyss"

while on ahead I know myself, with all, to be rushing
breakneck toward a future going, even Bach's last fugue
cut off midway, genius meeting its end before the ending?

"All the sounds of created being," you said, "are fused"
without confusion, everything sustained in a single note
until all the powers of the soul resound, now composed

into an "ineffably simple vibration," the one, no doubt,
you believed St. Francis heard, bewitching and seraphic.
You heard it in the rucked clamor of trench and redoubt

and from it divined the score—orchestral, symphonic—
of a milieu enfolding, unfolding. *It must be so*, you held
like Beethoven of his quartet. For "either there is escape,

somewhere, for thought and personality, or the world
is a tremendous mistake." Decades now, you are gone
into that ascendant heart, while in my neighbor's yard

a latticework of clematis riots purple blue—star-womb
on the trellis, risen, ecstatic, sustaining another spring,
an astonishment of beauty transfigured from the random.

Teach me to see in all this divergent errancy something
of your fullness. Teach me to listen, to hear, one chord
of the unfinishable, so that I, too, might enter the song.

Ψ

Bless me father, it is as you said: dead end or open road.
Let it be the road that calls to one across the bottomless,
no metaphor, no bridge, but matter's own seething tide

that ventures every path in faith despite all faithlessness
where entropy, complexity, your two opposing currents,
compose the deep. What I see in this endless genesis

is like the snapshot of a wave, not the long emergence,
as when a fog of raw happenstance diffuses into flow
and what flows there is spirit, source of the confluence

even at the first flash and its billowing, a blazing glow
of particles cooling to atoms, cooling then to galaxies—
pinwheel eddies of dust spiraling, the whole tableau

a turbulence of things gathered to thrum and tapestry.
Blink ten billion years—a first cell. Blink billions more
and out of chemical death, what? Larger lives, catalysis,

gene-communal collusions, jostle of prey, predator,
shell and fin, hush-uplift of lung belaboring to land,
fritterings of wings in leaves, eggs under the conifer,

dinosaurs and flowers, continents joined in slow dance
parting, with paws in dirt, a spread of feathers into sky,
before the deft-handed stranger steps upright in grass.

Let its end be on the way, a man walking unrecognized
where two friends travel, grieving, to the evening town.
Stay with us, they offer, to the one who draws beside.

Ψ

The choice is ours, you believed, suicide or adoration
established the moment something altered the current,
like a river enriched, you said, by contact with the plain

until "the vital flux," now alluvial, crosses to reflection,
and what manifests to form is the enormous headlong
bloom of planetary mind—our monstrous inflorescence

pushing forward. Even the frailest smallest pitiable thing,
risen by coincidence, is provident, the fiat of the whole
woven through the manifold. So, what of our far-flung

march and throng—ill-starred disaster, or promised goal
toward which the living arrow flies from one extinction
to the next? Cambrian, Ordovician, Permian, Eocene,

Miocene: the way of things. Great-tusked wooly fauna
fell at our own pending hands, cast out. The last auk
strangled on Eldey. No one is an island (John Donne)

but the main is. I hear lost worlds sing inside the rock.
Desiccated corals. Bat middens in the Cave of Aeolus.
This by now long-swelling, surging flood of over-kill.

Father, I grow stone-eyed before the glut of rainforests
hacked, burned, evaporating glaciers, methane strayed
from permafrost, this wrong road away from Emmaus.

How to rise ahead amidst the sundering, heaving waste,
and you, most faithful, chiding our path to "total death"?
The elephants, dwindling, also mourn their dead at graves.

Ψ

Still, I would see with you, life's long spiral unscathed,
irreversible, your evolutive Logos, and we "like leaves,
buds from which everything appears in its proper place

and time," your nod to the *Origin*, its great living tree—
and suffering an "ascensional force" drawing our ends
forward, the Crucified's Vitruvian arms outreached

through all matter to "the farthest corners of creation."
But the figure's not a tree, it's a trellis for us humans,
our bloodlines from mitochondrial Eve recombinant

and the finer features of our Within, deeply wound,
is something like a tapestry, or some intricate mosaic
proving the bard's trope of one containing multitudes,

admixtures of others, each other, our inner alchemy
threading back to beginning, singular black hole
of our arrival, brought to presence with what comes:

corn from grass, tool in hand from the image of a tool
in mind—the kinship of things that do not look akin.
Why then *this* history: star clusters, spearhead routes,

the very genes suppressed by the Strong Man, simian
dreams spun by force of luck, the crosses crooked,
another knee on the neck, another future broken?

I look to the solace of bone flutes, lion-men carved
in mammoth tusks. And to the silenced ones, stone
circles, eagle talon jewelry in the more ancient caves.

Ψ

Bless me father, this house made of many mansions—
matter self-organizing, shaping itself into multitude,
shoreless sums of galaxies in a grain's breadth of sand

held up to the sky—expands into nothing inwardly,
no boundary, only the quickening volume of space
from laboratory stars, and like the negative around

a vase that dedicates the shape, the twin darknesses,
as if inferred from infrared, flowers there, unseen.
What am I, father, but one particle of consciousness

adrift, with others amidst this muddle of a species,
its prodigal numbers fast-forwarding in the crib?
In the mansion of the virus the limitless is *passé*—

bird-faced bloodletters, hawk-beaked with ambergris,
goggle glasses for eyes, hover among the suffering,
their long robes suddenly rubberized, make-shifted

into spacesuits, scrubs, as out of each raw throat juts
the winding transparent branch—blunt harbinger
of the metamorphosis, crux of your last penumbra:

for "evil is inevitable in the course of a universe
that evolves in time." Once in gold Egyptian light
you saw the range like a sawblade, Sinai's massif,

a horizon like a knife edge along the lowering sky.
Today, my garden keeps faith in its fragile tillage—
larkspur, sage, salvia, dead nettle, creeping thyme.

Ψ

And lilac banks, lavender on the Chara-Ousso-Gol—
where you said "world does not move at random,
nor does it mark time, but even inside its turmoil

the universe is growing. Something is being made."
So, out of quantum haze, vesicles, electron spins
ripened in the gulf between beholder and beheld

as if cohered by decoherence here: this cyclamen
germinated from its central corm, the seedling
shoot unfolding upward into five curling petals,

these soft flames lifted out of variegated leaves—
sugar stencils of Christmas trees, or arrowheads
at the heart of every darkened opened palm, ivy-

shaped, each fastened to a cup, the petals curved
into auricles, little ears, that almost now appear
to be listening, in their way, to some song heard

on their own frequency, not mine: my *stargazer*,
cyclamen hederifolium, though the one life thrives
like the sun in fragments of a shattered mirror.

O how to see seeing in our intricate bright caves,
as if the eye could see itself, and the soul's beam
manifest like this flower born from infinite waves

of possibility, matter like dirt, a photon's dream
of scent, taste, touch. And in the empty space
across it all, light circuiting the seer and the seen.

Ψ

Bless me father, a roll of the loaded chemical dice
fashioned the fourfold language of a cell that read
itself, the root, *the route*, of life at watch, miraculous.

To perceive what is chance and divined as a braid,
as communion, God's long disclosure, longed for,
of a still deeper double life of God and the world,

until universe and earth align—an intelligent mirror
of All, all-in-all—I believe is what you ask of me.
Today, I read how the manakin's wing feathers whir,

strum, bow like a violin with such resonant speed
they stridulate to F sharp/G, the bird's wing-song
a brilliant come hither to its mate. It is only beauty

happening again, as it does, with utter decadence,
like the argus's golden spheres, or the peacock's
eyespots that Darwin saw as scandal to selection—

as if threads of superabundance were now at work,
aesthetics over function, or the teleology of play,
and everything evolving in beauty for beauty's sake.

Which is not to say that the hawk, imperturbable
on its bough, and the murder with its urgent caws,
portends no *mene mene* of the incomplete or fallen.

Matter as host and cross is what invites my awe,
the way the saint at chapel this time took the bread
and resolved, at once, that all he'd known was straw.

Ψ

And if I take today, father, Cusa's "De li Non-Aliud"
I do to know the riddle of your vision of the heart,
God as "Not-Other," God at once home and road—

and end that makes all, not other than what they are:
what you called the common heart of things, its glow
in dawn-light, and "in the flesh" a burning bush on fire

by "light from light" shining forth through broken glass,
back beyond knowing's corona, its slow event horizon.
Like the man from *The City of God* I, too, am restless,

having trailed the sprawling venture of my kind into
the vector of our currency. Now, in the meantime,
I look out to a billowing above a ridge, to the front

moving in on the edge—the boundary of a striving,
or is it just depthless seething, not your one gesture
of creation reaching out across the fullness of time?

On the day that you died, Easter, they found a prayer
to the savior's heart, parted open, crowned, aflame
as on my own long-worn-thin childhood scapular.

What I see burning now are great forests set ablaze
across a world-wide net, thought's pale simulacrum,
dull image of your species' mindful web. These days,

I long to see myself in limestone hills, a quiet walk
on fossil reefs raised up, to know God is not-other
than a winter-quickened orchid flowering in its crack.

Ψ

Bless me father, shall I consider for the figure of your
irresistible Vortex, which spins into its Life the infinite
stuff of things, the reality of God as divine attractor:

like a bob pendulum whose apparently chaotic orbit
draws everything into pattern, order, butterfly & flow,
neither turbulence nor equilibrium: which, in the circuit

of its emergence, everything likewise emerges in tow,
like eyes arising from water, spirals, waves, to become
organs in dynamic frames in which we know we know?

Above our siphoned atmosphere, great mirrors home
their lattice honeycomb for the most ancient light,
pillars risen, creational, in a nebula's gaseous womb,

gradient rays, red-shifting galaxies in the blank fields
where-when the first far clusters lens into presence,
each a glittering broach pinned spinning to the veil.

Now look down into an inner sky where the electron
keeps pace with the timeless until I bend and find
its many paths in an instant converging to only one.

In this double vision—double of eternity and time—
the fontal stays, hidden, an image glimpsed, a trace,
that I know to be my own, but distant, unrealized,

and drawn by loving hands from the vagrant source.
What Someone sees my seeing in this desire I seek?
You looked into creation's dust and saw a radiant Face.

Ψ

Bless me father, what is
this humming of strings
as though a single chord were

this joyous singing inside the rock,
from fractal mountains, fractal seas
perpetually struck and struck

woven with the depths,
the rhythm of all movement
from hydrogen and helium

to register the highest keys,
from flash to primal nuclei,
the dawning of transparency

into stars and elements
order in broken symmetry,
that wakens to a warmth of suns

evolving out of raging ties,
the supernova's cauldron womb
birthing ten billion billion skies

that rise inside a single cell
and draws the living fountain on
before still more derive from two

and trip the inexhaustible looms
to make the furnace flicker green
and the many begin to roam

under waves and out of them
where thriving and extinction turn
helices winding from the past

into a pageantry of scenes
like interleaving counterpoints,
in which the future comes to be,

while every fleeting now escapes
the very word that time desires,
and to enter, if only passingly,

before an instant's praise anoints
the seam that holds the emptiness
some beholding, however faint,

the light you lived your life for
you came to that last Easter day,
your world-line confirmed the point,

the threshold of the radiance
shaft blazing as into a cavern
Omega bred from alphas of chance,

and chance gamed in emergence,
here before all and hidden in all
like glitter ascending into fire—

the dice loaded by dint of One
who spurs all on ahead in flight,
flesh flashing a path through stone—

Some wellspring of creation, lithe in the scattered sunlight—
it pours itself at dawn along this single inlet shore
the rising sun being born, center of deep delight

at the heart of the world, and the water a mirror
entirely reflecting sky. Here again is your paten,
here again your chalice in the vessel of matter

in which the All is emptied, nothing abandoned.
Beyond these harbor islands, it is the human city,
visible from the tidal hallows here at World's End

that feels like the passing planet we must grieve
right now, now that the planet, too, has risen.
Let me hold in my gaze some filament of eternity.

———

Let me hold in my gaze some filament of eternity,
right now, now that the planet, too, has risen
that feels like the passing planet we must grieve.

Visible from the tidal hallows here at World's End,
beyond these harbor islands, it is the human city
in which the All is emptied, nothing abandoned,

here again your chalice in the vessel of matter
entirely reflecting sky. Here again is your paten
at the heart of the world, and the water a mirror—

the rising sun being born, center of deep delight.
It pours itself at dawn along this single inlet shore,
some wellspring of creation, lithe in the scattered sunlight...

...as the roaming mind recalls its home
at the end of distances, the uncreated

waking as from the most vivid sleep
when the light flowers out of its now

into the most ancient sky, All Being
Becoming All, eternally quickening to...

NOTES AND ACKNOWLEDGMENTS

The three "books" of *The Mansions* should be read as three "world lines." In physics, a world line is a curve in spacetime that tracks a particle over the course of its existence. Sections from *The Mansions* have appeared in the following journals: *Alabama Literary Review, Berfrois, Bluestem, FEKT, The Hudson Review, Ibbetson Street, Image, Irish Pages, JMWW, Literary Matters, Long Poem Magazine, Notre Dame Review, Ocean State, Pennine Platform, Plume, Prairie Schooner, Presence, River Styx, Ruminate, Spiritus,* and *Tiferet*. Selections from "At the Grave of Teilhard de Chardin" appeared in the anthology *A Given Grace* (Squircle Line Press, 2021).

ONE: FROM NOTHING

From Nothing would not have been written without the generous support of a fellowship in poetry from the John Simon Guggenheim Foundation and Four Way Books which provided a month-long residency at the Fine Arts Work Center in Provincetown. First published by Four Way Books in 2016, *From Nothing* won the Julia Ward Howe Award in Literature.

Three works were essential to the making of this poem: John Farrell's *The Day Without Yesterday: Lemaître, Einstein, and the Birth of Modern Cosmology*, Dominque Lambert's *L'Itinéraire Spirituel de Georges Lemaître*, and Valérie de Rath's *George Lemaître, le Père du Big Bang*, as well as Lemaître's own writings and notebooks. *From Nothing* would not have been written without the enormous generosity and personal attention of Liliane Moens-Haulotte; Director of the Archives Georges Lemaître at the University of Louvain La Neuve, Belgium; her husband Michel Haulotte; Gilbert Lemaître who provided important insight into his uncle's life; and Christine Casson who was instrumental in assisting with the research as well as offering inspiration and an impeccable ear. *From Nothing* is dedicated to them. I am also grateful for the helpful readership of Bruce Beasley, Hamida Bosmajian, Martha Rhodes, William B. Thompson and William Wenthe.

The Most Ancient Light in the Most Ancient Sky (Sections I-XI)—is from Wallace Stevens's "Ordinary Evening in New Haven." *The Death of One God Is the Death of All* (XII-XXII) is from Stevens' "Notes Toward a Supreme Fiction;" and *Of Motion the Ever-Brightening Origin* (XXIII-XXXIII) is from Stevens' "The Auroras of Autumn." The quotation preceding *The Most Ancient Light in the Most Ancient Sky* is from Georges Lemaître's "The Primeval Atom;" the quotations preceding The *Death of One God Is the Death of All* are from Albert Einstein's *Life and Opinions*; the quotation preceding *Of Motion the Ever-Brightening Origin* is from Pascal's *Pensées*.

SECTIONS

(Fountain)
Perihelion: point of orbit of a planet when it is nearest the sun; *Cepheid*: variable or pulsating star whose luminosity helps chart distances in space. The lines in italics are paraphrased from Lemaître's early essay on the primeval atom.

(Origin)
Lemaître's father, Joseph, owned a factory in Charleroi, 173 miles south of Brussels. He invented a new procedure for "stretching" glass. When the factory was destroyed, he borrowed from family to pay back his employees and creditors after which he moved the family to Brussels and practiced law.

(Fiat)
Lemaître fought in the Battle of the Yser, one of the most horrific of the First World War. For meritorious service, he received the Croix de Guerre.

(De Rerum)
Jules Henri Poincaré (1854-1912): French mathematician, physicist, and engineer who, among many innovations, introduced the modern concept of relativity.

(Parallax)
Introibo ad altare Dei. Ad Gloriam: In the Latin Mass, "I will go to the altar of God," "To the glory of." *Karl Schwarzschild* (1873-1916), German physicist, provided the Schwarzschild solution for rotating masses anticipating black hole theory; *Henry Moseley* (1887-1915), English physicist, famous for Moseley's law on the X-ray spectra that helps organize the chemistry of the periodic table according to physical law; *Willem de Sitter* (1872-1934), Dutch mathematician whose so called De Sitter Universe provides a cosmological model for Einstein's general relativity requiring a universe without matter.

(Trajectory)
Puranas: ancient Sanskrit religious text sacred to Hindus and Buddhists; Arthur Eddington (1882-1944), English physicist and earlier champion of relativity theory and Lemaître's theory of the "primeval atom;" *Sobral, Príncipe*: destinations for the 1919 expeditions for the solar eclipse which proved Einstein's prediction of relativity theory correct; *Bottom:* character in Shakespeare's *A Midsummer's Night's Dream*.

(Scope)
Harlow Shapely (1885-1972), American astronomer, who initially believed nebulae were part of the Milky Way and not galaxies in their own right; *Vesto Slipher* (1875-1969), American astronomer.

(Vector)
Erwin Schrödinger (1887-1961), German physicist and biologist and one of the founders of quantum mechanics, famous for Schrödinger's equation establishing the "wave function" of matter illustrated by the famous thought experiment known popularly as "Schrödinger's Cat."

(Proscenium)
Albert Einstein (1879-1955); *Solvay:* conference on physics and chemistry held in Brussels, 1927.

(Observance)
Edwin Hubble (1889-1953), American astronomer who discovered the degree of Doppler shift (red shift) is directly proportional to the speed at which galaxies are speeding away from the earth, thereby establishing the fact that the universe is expanding; *Milton Humason* (1891-1974), American astronomer.

(Shore)
The excerpts are from Einstein's *Ideas and Opinions* (New York: Crown, 1982).

(Melisma)
Hitler's mountain residence was in Berchtesgaden. On November 19, 1940, King Leopold of Belgium officially capitulated to the German Reich.

(Calculus)
Kurt Asche (1909-1998) oversaw the deportation of Belgian Jews to Auschwitz at the Micheline internment camp north of Brussels; *Jozef-Ernest van Roey* (1874-1961): Belgian Cardinal who publically opposed Nazi Germany and encouraged resistance against the occupying forces.

(Chamber)
Pope Pius XII, Eugenio Pacelli (1876-1958): controversial figure whose decisions during the Second World War to avoid direct confrontation with Hitler have caused him to be condemned in some quarters, while other scholars have praised his work to save Jews covertly without inciting further violence or endangering the Catholic Church; Jews were required to wear yellow stars in Nazi occupied Europe. Details from this section are derived from José Sánchez's even-handed book *Pius XII and the Holocaust.*

(Aperture)
The first thought experiment is posed by Frank Close in his book *The Void*; *Gregor Mendel* (1822-1884): Augustinian Monk, founder of the science of genetics.

(Tenebrae)
The first stanza riffs a phrase from Brian Greene's *The Elegant Universe*; *Der Alter*: "The Old One," Einstein's preferred appellation for God; *Newton's Divine Observer*: Sir Isaac Newton speculated that space might be filled with a spiritual substance and called space "the divine observatory."

(Sanctum)
Jan van Ruysbroeck fourteenth century mystic and author of *The Spiritual Espousals* and *The Sparkling Stone* (among other works) from which these paraphrases are taken.

(Imago)
Heisenberg's uncertainty principle maintains that in binaries of physical properties, the more one property is measured the less the other property can be determined—light behaving as either wave or particle but not both simultaneously; the lines in italics are taken from Erwin Schrödinger's *What Is Life?* The translation from the French is: "Eternal light engulfing all…a mysterious heat." In his notebooks, Lemaître copied and offered commentary on extensive passages from Ruysbroeck's writings.

(Repertory)
The species Homo sapiens emerges about 160,000 years ago, so about 5000 generations; Lemaître was a devotee of Molière's plays, but believed the plays to have been written in fact by Louis XIV; *forma omnium, materia omnium, / essentia omnium, omnia sunt in ipsa divina essential*: "the form of things," "the matter of things," "the essence of things" "all things exist in the very essence of God"—these are each theological formulas articulating God's relation to creation, as discussed in Józef Życiński's *God and Evolution*; the quotation at the bottom of the page is from Ruysbroeck's *The Spiritual Espousals*.

(Signature)

Apart from the biblical quotation in the first stanza the remaining italicized phrases are taken from Lemaître's archives at the university of Louvain-la-Neuve. The quoted lines are from Schrödinger's *What Is Life*. Lemaître's house was bombed inadvertently by U.S. warplanes in 1944; he narrowly escaped with his life; *Ananke*: Greek for "necessity."

(Veil)

J. Robert Oppenheimer (1904-1967) presided over the development of the atomic bomb during the Second World War, known as the Manhattan Project. Rapid Rupture was his code name; *Lieutenant General R. Leslie Groves* (1896-1970), military director of the Manhattan Project; *Jean Tatlock* was Oppenheimer's lover before and after his marriage; she committed suicide in 1944 after introducing Oppenheimer to Donne's "Holy Sonnets"; *Robert Christy* (1916-2012), American astrophysicist; *Tabor*: mountain in Israel and site of the biblical transfiguration of Jesus.

(Fractal)

Rue de Braekeleer is in Brussels, Belgium.

(Stream)

Fatima: The Feast of Our Lady of Fatima, May,13, commemorating the apparitions of the Virgin Mary in Portugal in 1917; *Coimbra*: observatory in Portugal; *Galilean coordinates*: after Galileo, coordinates used to transform between two reference frames in space. The word Galilean also has another intended incidental reference.

(Nexus)

After the Second World War, Lemaître was asked to join the Institute for Advanced Studies at Princeton to join Einstein and other notable scientists; he declined out of deference to taking care of his elderly mother. Kurt Gödel (1906-1978), Austrian mathematician and philosopher, and Niels Bohr (1885-1962), Danish physicist and one of the founders of quantum mechanics, spent time with Einstein at the Institute for Advanced Studies in Princeton; the first observation sketches the "three body problem in physics; *Planck threshold*: the Planck length is the tiniest unit of physical reality, named after Max Plank (1858-1947), German physicist; Blaise Pascal (1623-1662), French mathematician and philosopher. The quotation in the last stanza of this section is from his *Pensées*.

(Contratemps)
The opening stanza paraphrases Pius XII's speech to the Pontifical Academy of Sciences.

(Agnus)
George Gamow (1904-1968), Russian physicist who championed the idea of an expanding universe and discovered, among other things, the process by which hydrogen atoms decay, thereby presaging the inflation theory of universal expansion developed by Alan Guth. It is said he never used articles when he spoke in English.

(Anthropic)
Max Born (1882-1970), German physicist and developer of quantum mechanics. The lines in quotation paraphrase the recollection of one of Lemaître's students at the retreat.

(Cinema)
Hermann Bondi (1919-2005), German-born physicist and mathematician; Thomas Gold (1920-2004) Austrian-born physicist; and Fred Hoyle (1915-2001), English physicist, developed the steady state theory of the universe after watching the English film, *Dead of Night* in 1946. Hoyle and Lemaître traveled in Italy together in 1957, recounted in Hoyle's memoir, *Home Is Where the Wind Blows*.

(Spiritus)
Pascaline: the name of given by Blaise Pascal to the mechanical calculator he invented in 1642; Newton's "miracle pin": Sir Isaac Newton envisioned the precise calibration of the universe as a pin balancing precisely on the smooth surface of a mirror. I affiliate that precision with the concept of Logos, which also has religious implications; *spar-*

kling stone: title of Ruysbroeck's mystical treatise, from the biblical Book of Revelation 2: 17; *Hoc est corpus*: Latin for "This is my body," the words recited by the priest he raises the host in the Tridentine Mass; *riffraff*: Old English word for "particles"; *yelm*: Old English word for "substance" used by George Gamow for the early plasma of the universe.

(Corpus)

"Thinking reeds" is Pascal's phrase. In the early 1960s the University of Louvain faced a crisis when the Flemish students and faculty wanted to separate into a Dutch-speaking university, reflecting long-standing historical conflicts in Belgian society between French-speaking Walloons and the Flemish. Lemaître supported keeping the university together. The windows of his house were smashed with bricks in protest. The Catholic of University of Leuven became entirely Dutch-speaking in 1968; Louvain-la-Neuve began construction in 1971.

(Canto)

The opening lines paraphrase Augustine's *Confessions*; *Deus creator omnium*: "God that created all things," a hymn for Saturday vespers; Arno Penzias (1933), American physicist born in Poland, who with James Wilson (1914-2000) discovered the cosmic background microwave radiation in 1964 while working at Bell Labs in New Jersey. Penzias's father owned a leather business in Poland before escaping with his family. The italicized lines in the final stanza also paraphrase Augustine's *Confessions*.

(Matins)

Van Severen: Joris Van Severen (1894-1940), was a close friend of Lemaître's in the trenches of World War I and became a vocal member of the Front Movement of Flemish soldiers who were ardent Flemish nationalists. They both shared a Catholic faith inspired by Leon Bloy (1846-1917), the French religious philosopher and advocate for the poor. Van Severen and Lemaître's friendship dissolved as Van Severen became more radical in his politics, eventually gravitating to right wing sympathies. He was executed in 1940 by French soldiers.

(Cove)

The first line riffs Arnold Penzias's recollection of hearing the CMB, the cosmic microwave background radiation; the italicized lines are paraphrased from the final interview given by Lemaître two weeks before his death.

TWO: THIS BROKEN SYMMETRY

The life of Simone Weil as portrayed in "This Broken Symmetry" draws significantly from details and encounters offered in Simone Pétrement's definitive biography, *Simone Weil: A Life*. The poem also draws and adapts phrases from Simone Weil's own writings as rendered in *The Simone Weil Reader, Waiting for God, Gravity and Grace*, and *Lectures on Philosophy*. The three division titles are phrases taken from Wallace Stevens's poem "The Man with the Blue Guitar." The epigraph preceding "The Bread of Time to Come" is from *Waiting for God*, and preceding "A Native in the World" is from *Gravity and Grace*. "This Broken Symmetry" begins shortly after her death and ends some months before her birth. Sections from "This Broken Symmetry" won the Stephen J. Meringoff Award from the Association of Literary Scholars, Critics, and Writers. I am also grateful for the helpful readership of Hannah Matheson, Martha Rhodes, Aidan Rooney, and William B. Thompson.

SECTIONS

(Bybrook)

Bybrook Cemetery, where Simone Weil was laid to rest, is not far from Ashford Sanitarium where she died, August 14, 1943.

(Roots)

Charles de Gaulle (1890-1970). French general and politician who led the resistance against the Nazi occupation, and later founded the Fifth Republic party under which he was elected President of France from 1959 to 1969.

(Riverside)
André Weil (1906-1998). Brother of Simone Weil, celebrated mathematician known for his contributions to number theory and algebraic geometry. Caspar David Friedrich (1774-1840), German painter of the Romantic period. The lines ending this section are adapted from *The Bhagavad Gita*, the Laurie L. Patton translation.

(Font)
The lines ending this section are adapted from *The Bhagavad Gita*, the Laurie L. Patton translation.

(Anathema)
Father Perrin (1870-1942). Priest of the Dominican Order, close friend of Simone Weil. Their friendship and correspondences were essential to her spiritual development. *Anathema sit*: A form of excommunication, literally: "Let them be anathema."

(Le Poët)
Le Poët is located in the Jabron valley in the South of France. The Vitruvian man is a drawing by Leonardo da Vinci that depicts the human proportions in relation to geometry. The name comes from the writings of the Roman architect Vitruvius.

(Harvest)
Gustave Thibon (1903-2001) was a twentieth century French philosopher and 4-time Nobel nominee. He was influential to many writers, including Simone Weil, and later published her notebooks under the title *Gravity and Grace*.

(Montségur)
Montségur: A fortified French town, east of Bordeaux, build during the thirteenth century. The Cathars were followers of a Gnostic revival movement, persecuted by the Catholic Church. Pope Innocent III reigned from 1198-1216. An especially powerful pope, who believed the papacy's power was greater than that of empires and kings. The

last line alludes to Ezra Pound's troubadour poem, "Audiart," from Bertran de Born.

(Marmot)
The extended quotation in this section is adapted from Weil's words as reported in Simone Petrémont's *Simone Weil: A Life*.

(Rue de Catalan)
Selma Weil (1879-1965), Mother of Simone Weil.

(Dordogne)
Marcel Ravidat (1923-1995), discovered the cave paintings in Lascaux in 1940, one of the earliest known examples of Stone Age art.

(The Nail)
"Extreme affliction, which means physical pain, distress of the soul, and social degradation all at the same time, is a nail whose point is applied at the very center of the soul, whose head is all necessity, spreading throughout space and time." From *Waiting for God*.

(Rue de Fleurus)
Gertrude Stein (1874-1946) ran her famous salon out of her home at 27 Rue de Fleurus, not far from the Luxembourg Gardens, frequented by artists such as Picasso, Hemmingway, and Matisse. Many of the lines in this poem are adapted from Stein's writings. Baby Wojums (Alice B. Toklas) and Mama Wojums (Stein) were pet names the couple gave to each other. There is no evidence to my knowledge that Stein and Weil ever encountered each other in the Luxembourg Gardens.

(Gravity)
The final lines of George Herbert's "Love III" are woven into the final lines of this section. After reading Herbert's poem Weil reported having a mystical experience of Christ's presence.

(Solesmes)
The Solesmes Abbey is located in Sarthe, France.

(A Pythagorean Notion)
The figure of the tetrad (four) plays an important role in Plato's *Timaeus* and in new-Platonic thought. Vitruvian: see note above.

(Little Portion)
"The Canticle of Brother Sun and Sister Moon" is a religious song written by St. Francis, one of the earliest pieces of Italian literature.

(Firmament)
Galileo Galilee (1564-1642).

(Rue des Grand-Augustins)
Rue des Grand-Augustins is located in the Saint-Germain-des-Prés neighborhood of Paris, not far from the Luxemburg Gardens. Dora Maar: (1907-1997), French artist and lover of Pablo Picasso. There is no evidence to my knowledge that Picasso ever encountered Weil in or around the Luxembourg Gardens.

(Rio Ebro)
Los Picos Tres Marias, refers to "the peak of the three seas," the mountain source of the Rio Ebro in Spain.

(The Screen)
Weil believed Chaplin's film "Modern Times" captured the essence of the worker's plight. This section also references his film "The Great Dictator," his lampoon of Hitler.

(Processions)
After her year of factory work, Weil traveled with her parents to the Portuguese Coast. "No céu desponta nova luz" is a Portuguese hymn for the Nativity.

(A String)
This section lists names of factories where Simone Weil had been employed during her "Year of Factory Work"

(Papa Trotsky)
Bernard Weil (1872-1955), father of Simone Weil, was a prominent medical doctor who was raised in a Jewish family but grew distant from religion and gravitated to agnosticism. Natalia Sedova (1882-1962), the second wife of Leon Trotsky.

(Force)
See Simone Weil, "The Iliad: Poem of Force."

(Red Virgin)
Professor Célestin Bouglé (1870-1940) was a French philosopher and one of Simone Weil's teachers at the Ecole Normal. Le Puy was the location of her first teaching appointment.

(Rue Auguste Comte)
Location of the Weil apartment across from the Luxemburg Gardens. Auguste Comte (1798-1857) founded the doctrine of positivism.

(Martian)
Simone de Beauvoir (1908-1986), attended the École Normale with Simone Weil and Simone Antheriou. Alain (1868-1951), real name Èmile-Auguste Chartier, was Weil's inspirational teacher.

(Fable)
Alexander the Great (356 BCE-323 BCE)

(Tooth)
See note above for André Weil.

(Garden)
Watteau (1684-1721), founder of the Rococo Movement.

(Rue du Paradis)
The lines in italics are adapted from the Jewish Shema. The time of this section is Fall, 1908.

THREE: AT THE GRAVE OF TEILHARD DE CHARDIN

Circumstances, details, and personages from the life of Teilhard de Chardin included in the poem owe greatly to *Teilhard de Chardin: A Biographical Study* by Claude Cuénot, *The Life of Teilhard de Chardin* by Robert Speaight, and *The Spirit of Fire: The Life and Vision of Pierre Teilhard de Chardin*, by Ursula King, as do theological considerations developed by Robert Faricy, SJ in *The Spirituality of Teilhard de Chardin, Teilhard's Mysticism: Seeing the Inner Face of Evolution* by Kathleen Duffy, SSJ, and John F. Haught, *The New Cosmic Story*. *As in a Vivid Sleep* (Sections 1-XI) is from Wallace Stevens's "The Rock." *At the End of Distances* (XII-XXII) is from Wallace Stevens's "The Rock." *Like Glitter Ascended into Fire* (XXIII-XXXIII) is from Wallace Stevens's "The Sail of Ulysses." The epigraphs to *At the Grave of Teilhard de Chardin* are from Schrödinger's "Mind and Matter" and Teilhard de Chardin's "Letter to Abbé Breuil, 19 March 1934." The epigraph to "As in A Vivid Sleep" is from *The Divine Milieu*. The epigraph to "As in a Vivid Sleep" is from Darwin's letter to J.D. Hooker, 12 July 1870. The epigraphs to "Like Glitter Ascended into Fire" are from *The Divine Milieu* and Senghor's "Negritude: A Humanism of the Twentieth Century." I am also grateful for the helpful readership of Christine Casson, Hannah Matheson, and Aidan Rooney.

SECTIONS

(Stone)
Shortly after his death on Easter Sunday, 1955, Teilhard de Chardin was buried in the Jesuit Cemetery at St. Andrews-on-Hudson in Poughkeepsie, New York. Lines 10-12 are adapted from Teilhard's work "Let Me Explain."

(Puy-de-Dôme)
An extinct volcano in Auvergne, France, visible from Sarcenat, Teil-hard's childhood home.

(Wake)
Teilhard traveled to Cairo in 1905 and taught there until 1908.

(The Weald)
Teilhard attended the Jesuit school at Ore Place in Hastings, England, from 1908-1912. He would often walk through the nearby Weald, from the Old English word for forest.

(A Moon on the Front)
Sidi, means "lord" in Arabic; A marabout is a holy man or teacher. Lines 16, 17, and 19 paraphrase Teilhard's reflections in *Hymn of the Universe* and *The Heart of Matter*.

(Shell)
Bright Angel and the Burgess Shale are locations of fossil deposits in the Grand Canyon and the Canadian Rockies, respectively.

(Lattice)
Teilhard conducted geological and paleontological research in and around Tientsin, China in 1923-1924, 1926-1927.

(Current)
The phrase in line 18 alludes to a statement made by Teilhard in *The Human Phenomenon*. Teilhard worked with Marcellin Boule at the Natural History Museum, Paris—his window faced the Jardin des Plantes.

(Garment and Corpus)
Line 21 alludes to an observation made by George Johnson in his book *Fire in the Mind*.

(Fault)
The italicized phrase in the final stanza is from *The Divine Milieu*.

(Celestial Mountains)
The Tien Shan Mountains stretch east to west, west to east across Eurasia. Teilhard encountered their majesty during his participation in the Croisière Jaune in 1931.

(Hands)
George Barbour (1890-1977), Scottish geologist and educator who joined Teilhard on many field trips in China, India, Java, and elsewhere. Teilhard proposed the concept of the noosphere, a planetary consciousness, as essential to the next burgeoning state of human and ultimately "ultra-human" development. The exchange alluded to in the final stanzas is recounted by Robert Speaight in *The Life of Teilhard de Chardin*.

(Fan and Spearhead)
Marguerite Teilhard de Chambon (1880-1959), educator, French writer under the name Claude Aragonnès, cousin and confidant to Teilhard de Chardin, particularly during the First World War when he began developing his ideas on evolution and theology.

(We Thinking Reeds)
Auguste Valensin (1879-1953), Jesuit philosopher and one of Teilhard's closes friends and confidents. Maurice Blondel (1861-1949), French philosopher. Edouard le Roy (1870-1954), French philosopher and mathematician. "We Thinking Reeds"—the phrase is Pascal's (see note under "From Nothing.")

(Ensemble)
Émile Licent (1876-1952), French natural historian and founder of the Being Museum (now the Tianjin Natural History Museum) where he worked with Teilhard de Chardin.

(Fig)
Cardinal Merry del Val (1865-1930), Spanish Cardinal named Vatican Secretary of State who stood in opposition to Teilhard's embrace of "modernism," and one of many who opposed publication of his re-

ligious works. His fable of the fig is actually adapted from Richard Dawkins's *The Selfish Gene*.

(Mirror)
Marguerite-Marie "Guigite" de Chardin (1883-1936), sister of Teilhard de Chardin who suffered from a chronic illness that confined her to bed much of her life. The painting alluded to in the section refers of Pieter de Hooch's "The Courtyard of a House in Delft" used by A. Zee in his book *Fearful Symmetry* to illustrate chirality, the mirror spinning motions of sub-atomic particles.

(Glass)
Bruno de Solages (1895-1983), Rector of the Catholic Institute of Toulouse and leader of the Catholic resistance to the Nazis in France, offering protection to Jews. Toulouse is known as "La Ville Rose" for its architecture. Teilhard's book *How I Believe* is a response to Bruno de Solages inquiry. Léon Bloy (1846-1917) French novelist and poet, who declared "everything is adorable," a motto Teilhard would repeat, though he had trouble believing.

(Labyrinth)
Gabriel Marcel (1889-1973), French Catholic existentialist philosopher, playwright, and musician critical of Teilhard's optimism for the species. The quotations in the third stanza are adapted from Teilhard's essay "Human Energy." The labyrinth described at the section's end is in Chartres cathedral.

(Thread)
Paul Valéry (1871-1945), French poet, essayist, and philosopher.

(Icon)
Lucile Swan (1890-1965), American sculptor and close confidant of Teilhard de Chardin. Sculpted the bust based on the skull of Sinanthropus. Details in this section owe their inclusion to *The Letters of Teilhard de Chardin and Lucile Swan*, edited by Mary Gilbert and Thomas King.

(La Cotte)
Teilhard lived on the Channel Island of Jersey from 1902-1905 after being forced out of France. His boat ride to the Neanderthal cave by an island fisherman is mentioned in Robert Speaight's, *The Life of Teilhard de Chardin*.

Like Glitter Ascended into Fire
Quotations included in the first section are adapted from *The Letters of Teilhard de Chardin*, edited by Pierre Leroy, SJ. The allusion to Bach's final work and death owes its presence to Roger Penrose's *The Emperor's New Mind*.

Some of the details in the second section are from my reading of *The Universe Story* by Brian Swimme and Thomas Berry.

Details in the third section were influenced by my reading of *The Sixth Extinction* by Elizabeth Kolbert.

Quoted material in the fourth section derives from Teilhard's, *The Human Phenomenon*. The swastika was originally the Hindu symbol for good fortune before its adoption by the Nazis. Details of the last three stanzas owe their presence to my reading of David Reich's *Who We Are, How We Got Here*.

The cosmogonic progression of the fifth section is informed by *The Universe Story*, Brian Swimme and Thomas Berry. The quoted material in the penultimate stanza is from Teilhard's *How I Believe*.

In the sixth section, the Chara-Ousso-Gol is a river in China, site of one of many field trips made by Teilhard. The quoted material is from *The Letters of Teilhard de Chardin*, edited by Pierre Leroy, SJ.

In the seventh section, "the fourfold language of a cell" refers to the four bases of the DNA molecule, ACTG (adenine, cytosine, guanine, thymine). Details in this section owe their presence to David Prum's, *The Evolution of Beauty*. *Mene, mene* is Aramaic for numbered, weighed; in the Book of Daniel, 5:25, the phrase *mene, mene, tekel, upharsin* is literally the writing on the wall that Daniel construed to mean God had weighed Belshazzar and his kingdom and had found them insufficient, and would level them.

The eighth section riffs the seminal philosophical / theological work of Nicholas of Cusa (1401-1464). The saint referred to in the third stanza is St. Augustine whose magnum opus was *The City of God*. "You have made us for yourself, and our hearts are restless until they find peace in you," Augustine reflected famously in his *Confessions*.

The image of the bob pendulum in the ninth section owes its presence to my reading of *Teilhard's Mysticism* by Kathleen Duffy who likewise envisions God as a divine attractor. The reflection on seeing at the section's end is influenced by Robert Wood's *Being and the Cosmos: Seeing and Indwelling*.

The cosmogonic progression in the tenth contrapuntal section alludes to observations made in *The Universe Story* by Brian Swimme and Thomas Berry. The form of a contrapuntal, readable simultaneously down each column and across each column, embodies an inherently trinitarian architecture.

The eleventh section alludes to Teilhard's "The Mass on the World." World's End is an isthmus and natural preserve in Massachusetts, south of Boston. I allude to Nazim Hikmet's great poem, "On Living," in this palindrome.

INDEX OF SECTIONS AND FIRST LINES

(Repertory) "The processional enters with its deliberate masques"
(Signature) "And the music of what happens? Hiss and battle strafe"
(Veil) "When they christened me secretly Rapid Rupture"
(Fractal) "And after the end the pat outbreak of rapture, the gone"

Of Motion the Ever-Brightening Origin
(Stream) "Jubilant billowing from the choir loft, throngs in song"
(Nexus) "To you even so comes the open door: to commune"
(Contratemps) "All one, one would believe, and *Behind Every Door*"
(Agnus) "Mary had little lambda. His fleece was Jesus—Ha!"
(Anthropic) "This process of coming to life: autocatalysis of wave"
(Cinema) "In the film that doesn't begin and never ends, a man"
(Spiritus) "Stylus, number wheel, gear tooth, cog, a falling weight"
(Corpus) "For all of it, how presumptuous, we thinking reeds"
(Canto) *"Is it motion itself that makes the day? Or is it the time"*
(Matins) *"Mon ami, mon frère*, in the trenches nearly *mon semblable"*
(Cove) "Sometimes it's no different than the sound of the surf"
"...*and the universe* nothing more than dream..."

TWO: THIS BROKEN SYMMETRY
The Bread of Time to Come
(Bybrook) "She adored sunsets, and her last was a flaming host"
(Roots) "He is waiting at the door of 'Miss Simone,' curled there"
(Decreation) "But to enter the uncreated, Nothing's naked open sea"
(Riverside) "Below the brownstone-solid bulwark of the Palisades"
(Font) "New York bound, a reek of diesel from its pluming stacks"
(Anathema) "She only reads what she hungers for, only when she has"
(Le Poët) "Not as in that Alpine photo below the chalet years before"
(Harvest) "Like someone who has spent long hours among the vines"
(Montségur) "High, high and sure, far above the poplars' spreading tips"

(Marmot) "And so, for a figure of the creature consider
   the marmot"
(Rue de Catalan) "Dear Monsieur, if one must be exiled one
   should have a view"

Exceeding Music
   (Dordogne) "Yes, Ravidat, to follow the rabbit down its
      winding hole"
   (The Nail) "Through the palm spread wide along the ruled
      beam jutting"
   (Rue de Fluerus) "War is not so very near even when it is near
      these fields"
   (Gravity) "To consider the storm trooper goose-stepping into Prague"
   (Solesmes) "Eggshell, bone, swan's fleece pearl: lactescent statuary"
   (A Pythagorean Notion) "Here, now: God the architect, God
      geometer. As on the icon"
   (Little Portion) "In the eye between the Anchluss and blood-fires
      of Guernica"
   (Firmament) "God's Adamic touch, the Banishment,
      Michelangelo's skin"
   (Rue des Grands-Augustins) "Between my first name and last, a
      litany of saints unfolds"
   (Rio Ebro) "After turning away from the rearguard of Paris, the safe"
   (Screen) "This flicker-shimmer in the cave's wide dark: a figure lifts"

A Native in This World
   (Processions) "Nascent silence. Above the sea, a full moon ripples
      its light"
   (String) "Not the village, south of Viana do Castello, not the
      blessing"
   (Papa Trotsky) "Dear L, It perhaps will not surprise you that the
      Bellevilles"
   (Force) "NOTHING ENTERS HERE THAT IS NOT
      GEOMETRY"
   (Red Virgin) "High on her volcanic spur above the city, coral-
      colored bronze"

(Rue Auguste Comte) "From the terrace, clockwise: Eiffel Tower, Chaillot, the dome"

(The Martian) "Simone et Simone—we met each other while we prepared"

(Fable) "Wind flower, anemone, summoned by the goddess's tears"

(Tooth) "A brother is like a tooth, Simone would say, a good thing"

(Garden) "These designs attributed to God are cuttings made by us"

(Rue du Paradis) "'I am giving birth to something' she'll declare, though now"

"...and Silence after, the exceeding music..."

THREE: AT THE GRAVE OF TEILHARD DE CHARDIN

As in a Vivid Sleep

(His Stone) "Again, this dawn-lit incandescence through the yew trees"

(Puy-de-Dôme) "The late foragers wouldn't know what to make of me"

(Wake) "If, as Plato dreamed, time is just a moving image"

(The Weald) "And if a *shaw* could speak what would it say, my name"

(A Moon on the Front) "At night, when I wake, I look a blind man's Cyclopic eye"

(Shell) "*Spira mirabilis*, miraculous spiral, and from the one"

(Lattice) "His wrestling with me is inside, though the errant"

(Current) "In this river's perpetual haste, I am already always"

(Garment and Corpus) "Most of what I wear no one can see, my nakedness"

(Fault) "I am the scandal inside the rock, the mist in bronze"

(Celestial Mountains) "Inside the great mirroring eye of my Heavenly Lake"

At the End of Distances

(Hands) "To fall forward stage by stage till the end of the world"

(Fan and Spearhead) "Like conifers in the Bois de Boulogne
    where he would walk"
(We Thinking Reeds) *"In its depths I saw gathered, bound by love,*
    the scattered leaves"
(Ensemble) "The language of wings even in the hold of my nets"
(Fig) "'I resign myself to the activity of a microbe,' he said"
(Mirror) "When I read the draft of his *Milieu*, I knew the mirror"
(Glass) "Our Lord said it truly: 'It is necessary scandals come'"
(Labyrinth) "What did my rival call them, this host of living forms?"
(Thread) "Where sails like doves flocked the ocean's glittering
    roof"
(Icon) "My precious: I loved the way he filled my name with light"
(La Cotte) "Not the grotto at Puerto Viesco, its red ochre paintings"

Like Glitter Ascended into Fire
    "Bless me, father. What is this old, shattering emptiness"
    "Bless me Father, it is as you said: dead end or open road"
    "The choice is ours, you believed, suicide or adoration"
    "Still, I would see with you, life's long spiral unscathed"
    "Bless me father, this house made of many mansions"
    "And lilac banks, lavender on the Chara-Ousso-Gol"
    "Bless me father, a roll of the loaded chemical dice"
    "And if I take today, father, Cusa's 'De li Non-Aliud'"
    "Bless me father, shall I consider for the figure of your"
    "Bless me father, what is this joyous singing inside the rock"
    "Some wellspring of creation, lithe in the scattered sunlight"
    "... as the roaming mind recalls its home..."

ABOUT THE AUTHOR

Daniel Tobin is the author of nine books of poems, *Where the World Is Made* (Middlebury College Press, 1999), *Double Life* (Louisiana State University Press, 2004), *The Narrows* (Four Way Books, 2005), *Second Things* (Four Way Books, 2008), *Belated Heavens* (Four Way Books, 2010), *The Net* (Four Way Books, 2014), *From Nothing* (Four Way Books, 2016), and *Blood Labors* (Four Way Books, 2018), which the *New York Times* and *Washington Independent Review of Books* named one of the Best Poetry Books of the year. His suite of versions of poems from the German of Paul Celan, *The Stone in the Air*, also appeared in 2018. He is the author of the critical studies *Awake in America* (University of Notre Dame Press, 2011), *Passage to the Center: Imagination and the Sacred in the Poetry of Seamus Heaney* (University of Kentucky Press, 1999), and *On Serious Earth* (Orison Books, 2019), as well as the editor of *The Book of Irish American Poetry from the Eighteenth Century to the Present* (University of Notre Dame Press, 2007), *Light in Hand: Selected Early Poems of Lola Ridge* (Quale, 2007), *Poet's Work, Poet's Play: Essays on the Practice and the Arts* (University of Michigan Press, 2008, with Pimone Triplett), and *To the Many: Collected Early Works of Lola Ridge* (Little Island, 2018), which received a Special Commendation from the Poetry Society (U.K.). Among his awards are the "The Discovery/The Nation Award," The Robert Penn Warren Award, the Robert Frost Fellowship, the Katharine Bakeless Nason Prize, the Massachusetts Book Award in Poetry, the Julia Ward Howe Prize, the Stephen J. Meringoff Award, and fellowships from the National Endowment for the Arts and the John Simon Guggenheim Foundation. He teaches at Emerson College in Boston.

PUBLICATION OF THIS BOOK WAS MADE POSSIBLE
BY GRANTS AND DONATIONS. WE ARE ALSO GRATEFUL
TO THOSE INDIVIDUALS WHO PARTICIPATED IN
OUR BUILD A BOOK PROGRAM. THEY ARE:

Anonymous (14), Robert Abrams, Michael Ansara, Kathy Aponick, Jean Ball, Sally Ball, Clayre Benzadon, Adrian Blevins, Laurel Blossom, Adam Bohannon, Betsy Bonner, Patricia Bottomley, Lee Briccetti, Joel Brouwer, Susan Buttenwieser, Anthony Cappo, Paul and Brandy Carlson, Dan Clarke, Mark Conway, Elinor Cramer, Kwame Dawes, Michael Anna de Armas, John Del Peschio, Brian Komei Dempster, Rosalynde Vas Dias, Patrick Donnelly, Lynn Emanuel, Blas Falconer, Jennifer Franklin, John Gallaher, Reginald Gibbons, Rebecca Kaiser Gibson, Dorothy Tapper Goldman, Julia Guez, Naomi Guttman and Jonathan Mead, Forrest Hamer, Luke Hankins, Yona Harvey, KT Herr, Karen Hildebrand, Carlie Hoffman, Glenna Horton, Thomas and Autumn Howard, Catherine Hoyser, Elizabeth Jackson, Linda Susan Jackson, Jessica Jacobs and Nickole Brown, Lee Jenkins, Elizabeth Kanell, Nancy Kassell, Maeve Kinkead, Victoria Korth, Brett Lauer and Gretchen Scott, Howard Levy, Owen Lewis and Susan Ennis, Margaree Little, Sara London and Dean Albarelli, Tariq Luthun, Myra Malkin, Louise Mathias, Victoria McCoy, Lupe Mendez, Michael and Nancy Murphy, Kimberly Nunes, Susan Okie and Walter Weiss, Cathy McArthur Palermo, Veronica Patterson, Jill Pearlman, Marcia and Chris Pelletiere, Sam Perkins, Susan Peters and Morgan Driscoll, Maya Pindyck, Megan Pinto, Kevin Prufer, Martha Rhodes and Jean Brunel, Paula Rhodes, Louise Riemer, Peter and Jill Schireson, Rob Schlegel, Yoana Setzer, Soraya Shalforoosh, Mary Slechta, Diane Souvaine, Barbara Spark, Catherine Stearns, Jacob Strautmann, Yerra Sugarman, Arthur Sze and Carol Moldaw, Marjorie and Lew Tesser, Dorothy Thomas, Rushi Vyas, Martha Webster and Robert Fuentes, Rachel Weintraub and Allston James, Abby Wender and Rohan Weerasinghe, and Monica Youn.